AF661634

Lil Legends

Uppercase Tracing & Vocabulary Book

Writing Practice for Kids

level 1

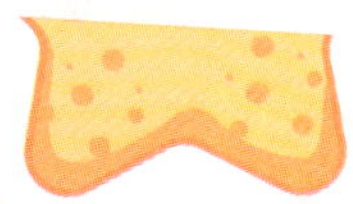

India's First Pre-Writing Program

OSWAAL BOOKS®

LEARNING MADE SIMPLE

Lil Legends

An imprint of Oswaal Books & Learning Pvt. Ltd.

PUBLISHED BY

OSWAAL BOOKS & LEARNING PVT. LTD.

INDIA OFFICE
1/11, Sahitya Kunj, M.G. Road,
Agra - 282002, (UP) India

UK OFFICE
1010, Cambourne
Cambridge, Cambridgeshire
CB 23#6DP, United Kingdom

Phone: 0562-2857671
E-mail: contact@oswaalbooks.com
Website: www.Oswaalbooks.com
ISBN: **9789357287036**
Printed at: Paras Offset Pvt. Ltd., Kundli-131028

©COPYRIGHT RESERVED BY THE PUBLISHERS

All rights reserved. No part of this book may be reproduced, stored in a retrieval system, or transmitted, in any form or by any means, without written permission from the publishers. The author and publisher will gladly receive information enabling them to rectify any error or omission in subsequent editions.

DISCLAIMER

This book is published by Oswaal Books and Learning Pvt Ltd ("Publisher") and is intended solely for educational use.
The Publisher expressly disclaims any liability for the use of, or references to, any terms or terminology in the book, which may not be considered appropriate or may be considered offensive, in light of societal changes. Further, the contents of this book, including references to any persons, corporations, brands, political parties, incidents, historical events and/or terminology within the book, if any, are not intended to be offensive, and/or to hurt, insult or defame any person (whether living or dead), entity, gender, caste, religion, race, etc. and any interpretation to this effect is unintended and purely incidental. While we try to keep our publications as updated and accurate as possible, human error may creep in. We expressly disclaim liability for errors and/or omissions in the content, if any, and further disclaim any liability for any loss or damages in connection with the use of the book and reference to its contents".

Uppercase Tracing & Vocabulary Book

Writing Practice for Kids

This Book Belongs to

....

Attention Parents...

Introducing India's first Pre-writing Program

Our proprietary writing program, is designed to help toddlers master their pre-writing skills. The program is based on five S-philosophies:

1. Skill Escalation:

All tracing opportunities advance in skill gradually, requiring one to follow the guide in its natural sequence. For example, letters with straight lines are explored before letters with zig-zag lines.

2. Strategic Sequence:

The program does not follow the traditional sequence of A, B, C but introduces tracing of letters in a strategic way that is best suited to the child's increasing skills and confidence. For example, L is introduced before letter A.

3. Smart Dot Guidance:

All patterns have smart guiding dots that are indicators on where to start, where to trace to and when one must lift off their writing instrument. All smart dots are numbered and coloured.

Starting Point: • (Green Dot)

End Point: • (Red Dot)

4. Stimulation based Practice:

The guide allows children to stay stimulated, and curious while practicing their writing skills. For example, children will get the opportunity to learn over 300 new picture based words.

5. Self- Appreciation:

The guide awards children with a certification to celebrate their learning and their enhanced writing skills.

Writing is an important tool, that must be introduced with great care and responsibility.

This guided pre-writing series is India's first pre-writing program that will allow parents and schools to simplify writing for their children and making pre-writing more structured, effective and fun. The program is aimed to help millions of toddlers to successfully yet responsibly embark on their writing journey.

Our goal in this series is to help parents:

- Learn about the age-appropriate grip goals for children
- Identify grip-appropriate writing instruments for children
- Embark on your child's writing journey in a structured and guided manner
- Simplify learning

Before we start on our child's writing journey, it is important that as parents and educators we are informed about some key developmental milestones.

What is a Pincer Grip? Why Do I need to know about it?

Pincer Grip is a grip between the index finger or middle finger and the thumb to grasp an object. Children are not born with this grip developed and first signs of development start around 9-10 months and this grip is fully developed around the age of 5-6 years.

TYPICAL PENCIL GRASP
DEVELOPMENT FOR HANDWRITING

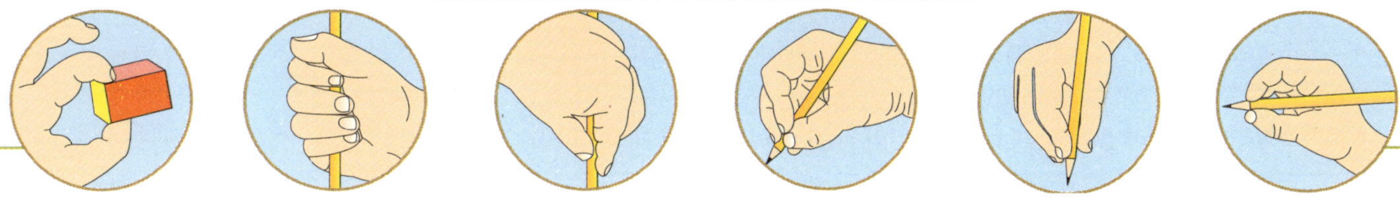

10 Months
Pincer Grasp | 12-15 Months
Palmar Supinate Grasp | 2-3 Years
Digital Pronate Grasp | 3-4 Years
Quadrupod Grasp | 3-4 Years
Static Tripod Grasp | 5-6 Years
Dynamic Tripod Grasp

What happens if a child is made to write before the grip is fully developed?

- Child may develop low self esteem and confidence incase unable to cope with writing.
- Child may become reluctant and unmotivated towards their learning.
- Child may adopt a poor handwriting.
- Child is often misdiagnosed with learning disorders, such as dysgraphia, dyslexia, due to their inability to cope with the existing writing programs, underdeveloped visual-motor skills.
- Causes muscle strain and potential loss of muscle dexterity.

Suggested activities to improve pincer grip development

- Pick and sort objects
- Tearing waste paper
- Pinching bubble wrap, clay, edible dough
- Lacing activities
- Squishing pomegranate, grapes and similar food items
- Open scribbling & mark making
- Colouring on vertical panel

"Before we ever put a pencil in a child's hands, those hands should dig, climb, press, push, squish, twist, and pinch in a wide array of environments and with a variety of materials."

Dr. Amanda Morgan, a world renowned early child expert.

Writing Instrument Guidelines

While their grips are still under development, children can participate in early writing by choosing the correct writing instruments:

• 10 months - 14 months: Ball Crayons (110 mm) & Jumbo Egg Chalk
• 15 months - 20 months: Grasp Crayons (33 mm), Fat Chalk, Dot Markers
• 21 months - 30 months: Grip Crayons (21 mm), Dot Markers, Golf Pencils With Triangular Grips
• 2.5 years - 3.5 years: Thick Crayons (11 mm), Golf Pencils With Grips
• 3.5 years - 4.5 years: Triangular or Hexagonal Pencils with Grip
• 4.5 years: Triangular or Hexagonal Pencils (Grip Optional)

Note: The listed width measurements of the recommended writing instruments are based after studying the effectiveness of the writing tools available for children.

You have picked Level 1: Uppercase Tracing & Vocabulary Book

This guide is focused on helping children start uppercase tracing & boosting their vocabulary.

(1) Letters are introduced in a strategic way to match the child's skill set.

(2) All letters are traced in a large and medium, age-appropriate, size format.

(3) Each child will be introduced with 12 associated words, allowing him/her to learn 310+ words.

(4) Smart dots and trace lines will guide the child to trace letters.

(5) Letters of a similar line construct are sectioned together.

Author Profile

Sonia Agarwal Bajaj

Sonia Agarwal Bajaj is a visionary new age edupreneur, who is making a profound impact in the field of education and skilling.

Sonia's passion to shape young hearts led her to start, Little Chipper International, an experiential learning based preschool in Agra. In a short span of time, this preschool has won many accolades and has been recognized amongst the top 5 Future Ready Preschools in India.

Committed to raising awareness about the importance of early education and helping parents embrace new learning and parenting techniques, Sonia hosts a spectrum of workshops across India. Her newest initiative includes conceptualising and authoring India's first structured pre-writing program for young children.

In addition to her contributions to the space in Early Education, she is the co-founder of Whiz league, an online skilling platform that offers celebrity led masterclasses at affordable prices. With over 1.2 million learning sessions, the platform grew to create its own learning management system that potentially helped hospitality and retail organizations train over 1 Lac staff members on a pan India basis. Sonia led the curriculum design and production for each of the 20 programs listed on the platform.

A Dhirubhai Ambani International School and Babson College alumnae, she has previously held a foray of responsibilities in the space of Ed-tech and fashion retail. Sonia has always been an advocate for the environment and she was a globally recognized founder of Whitenife, a platform that was dedicated to raising awareness on sustainable and ethical fashion.

With deep insight into the process and psychology of learning, Sonia is committed to further transform the education industry in times to come.

LEMONADE

LEAF

LOTUS

LETTUCE

LION

LOCK

LOVING LETTER L

TRACE OVER THE SMART DOTS TO MAKE LETTER L AND RECOGNISE THESE ASSOCIATED OBJECTS.

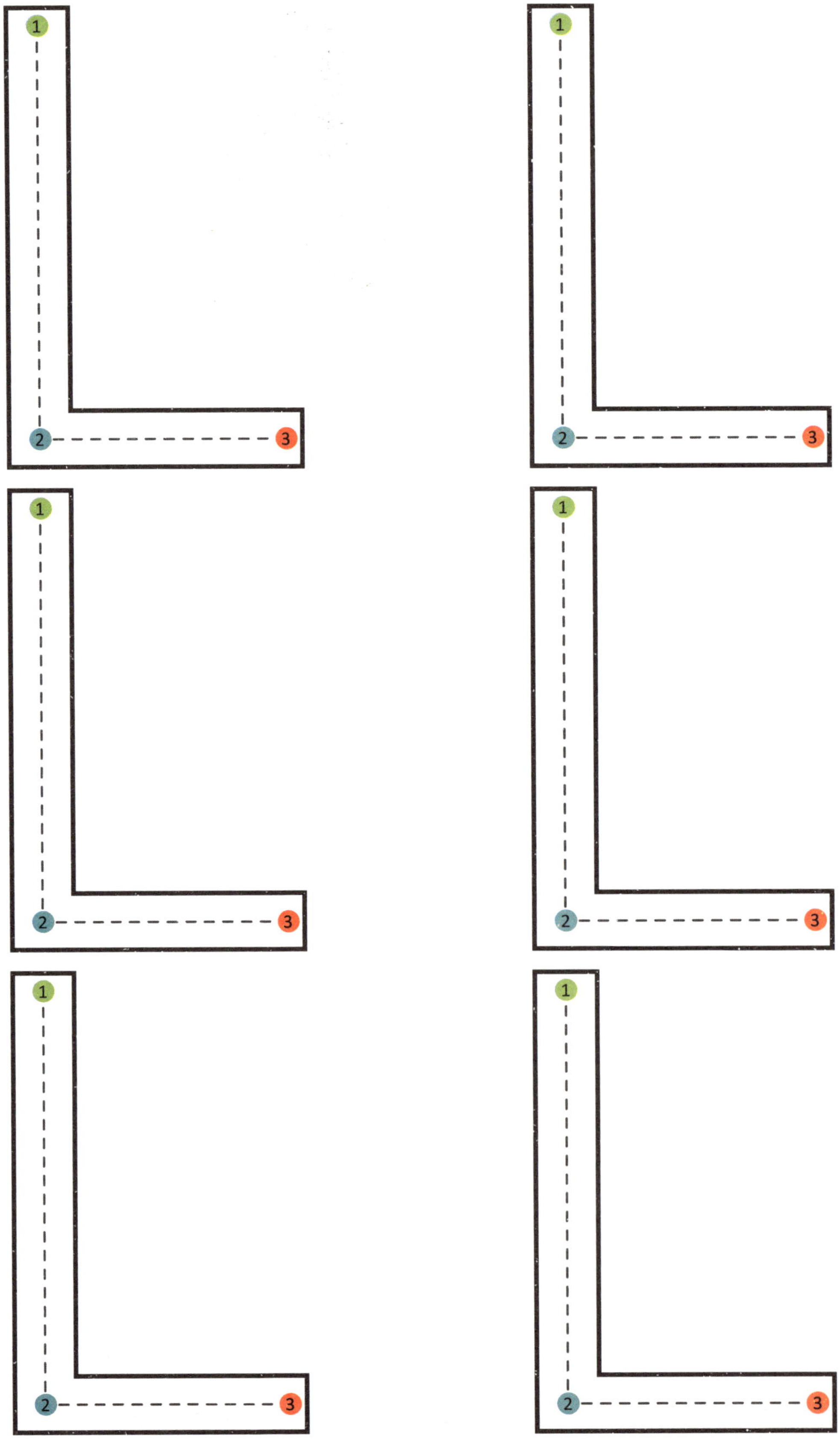

LOLLIPOP

LADYBUG

LAPTOP

LIZARD

LAMP

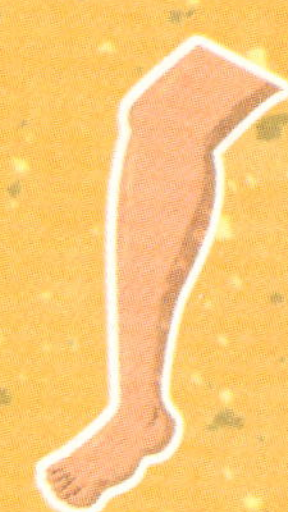
LEG

TOMATO

TREE

TABLE

TENT

TOOTHBRUSH

TEDDY

THRILLING LETTER T

TRACE OVER THE SMART DOTS TO MAKE LETTER T AND RECOGNISE THESE ASSOCIATED OBJECTS.

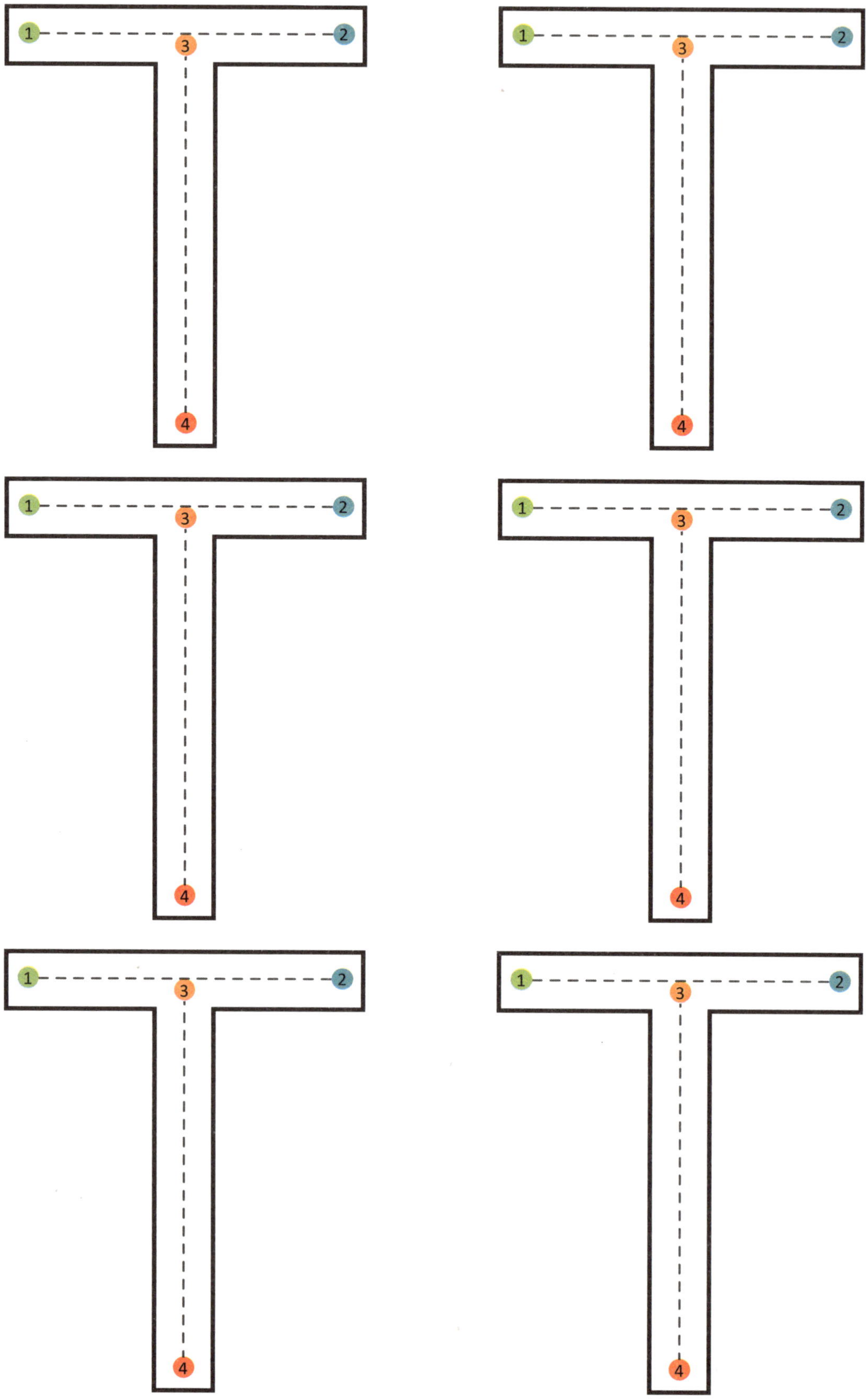

T-SHIRT

TRACTOR

TIGER

TEAPOT

TURTLE

TRAIN

INNOVATIVE LETTER I

TRACE OVER THE SMART DOTS TO MAKE LETTER I AND RECOGNISE THESE ASSOCIATED OBJECTS.

INSECTS

ICE

INKPOT

ICE-CREAM

IRON

INFANT

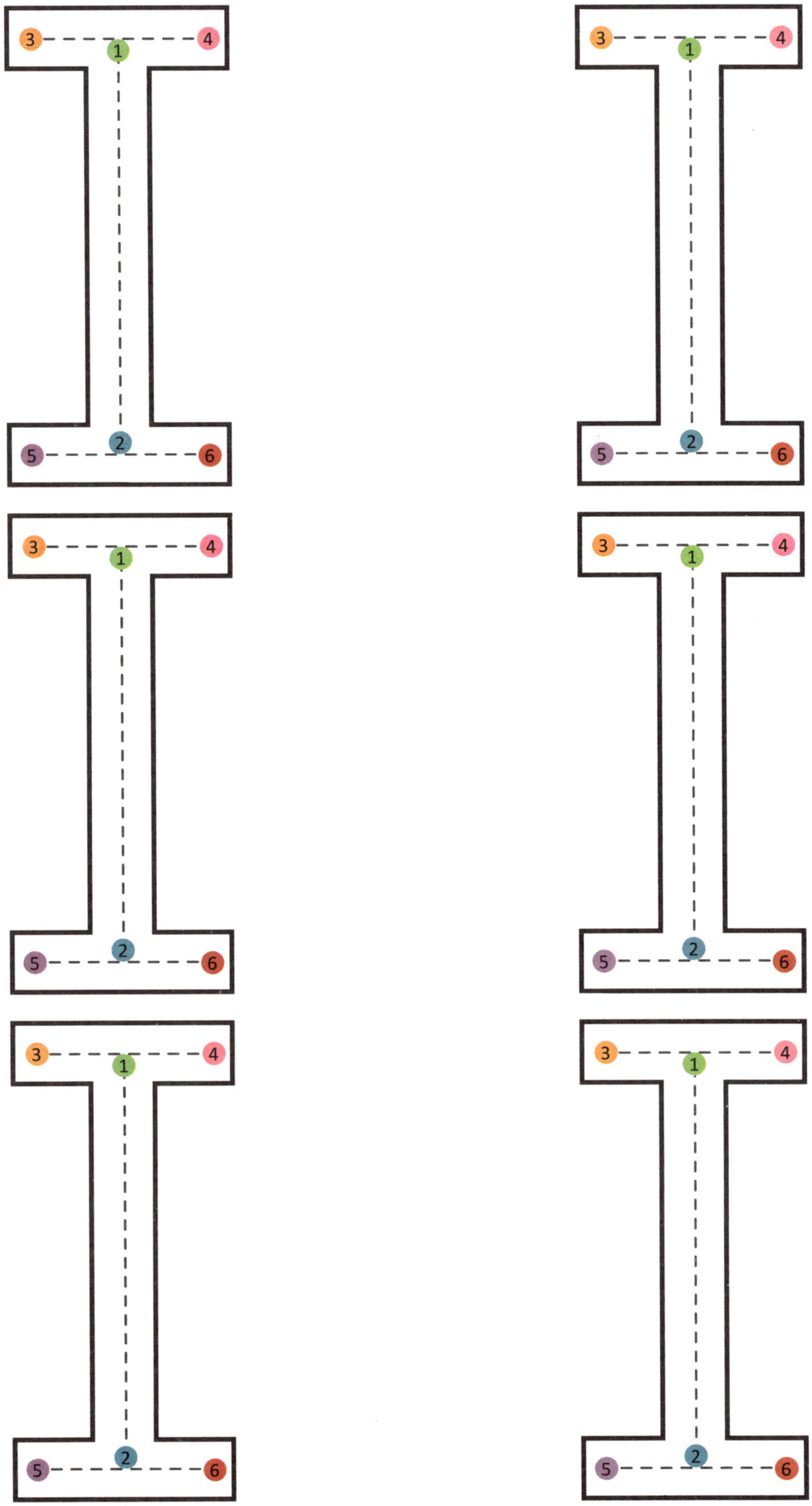

INDIA

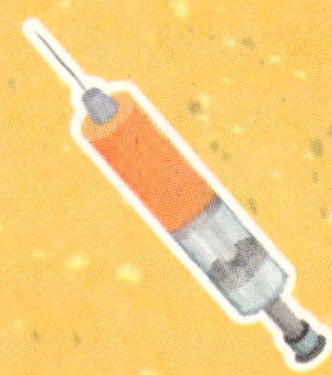

INJECTION

IGLOO

ITALY

IGUANA

INVITATION

EARTH

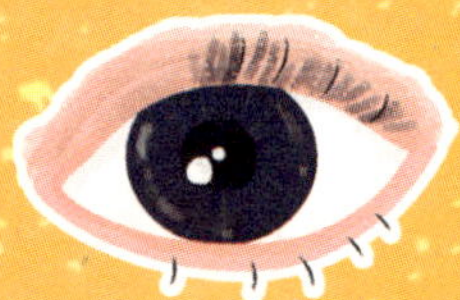

EYE

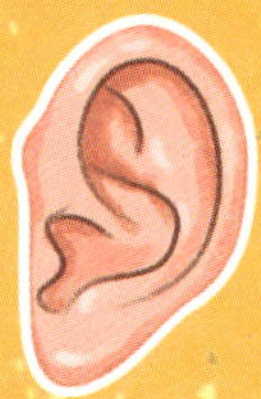

EAR

EARTHWORM

ENGINE

ERASER

EXCITED LETTER E

TRACE OVER THE SMART DOTS TO MAKE LETTER E AND RECOGNISE THESE ASSOCIATED OBJECTS.

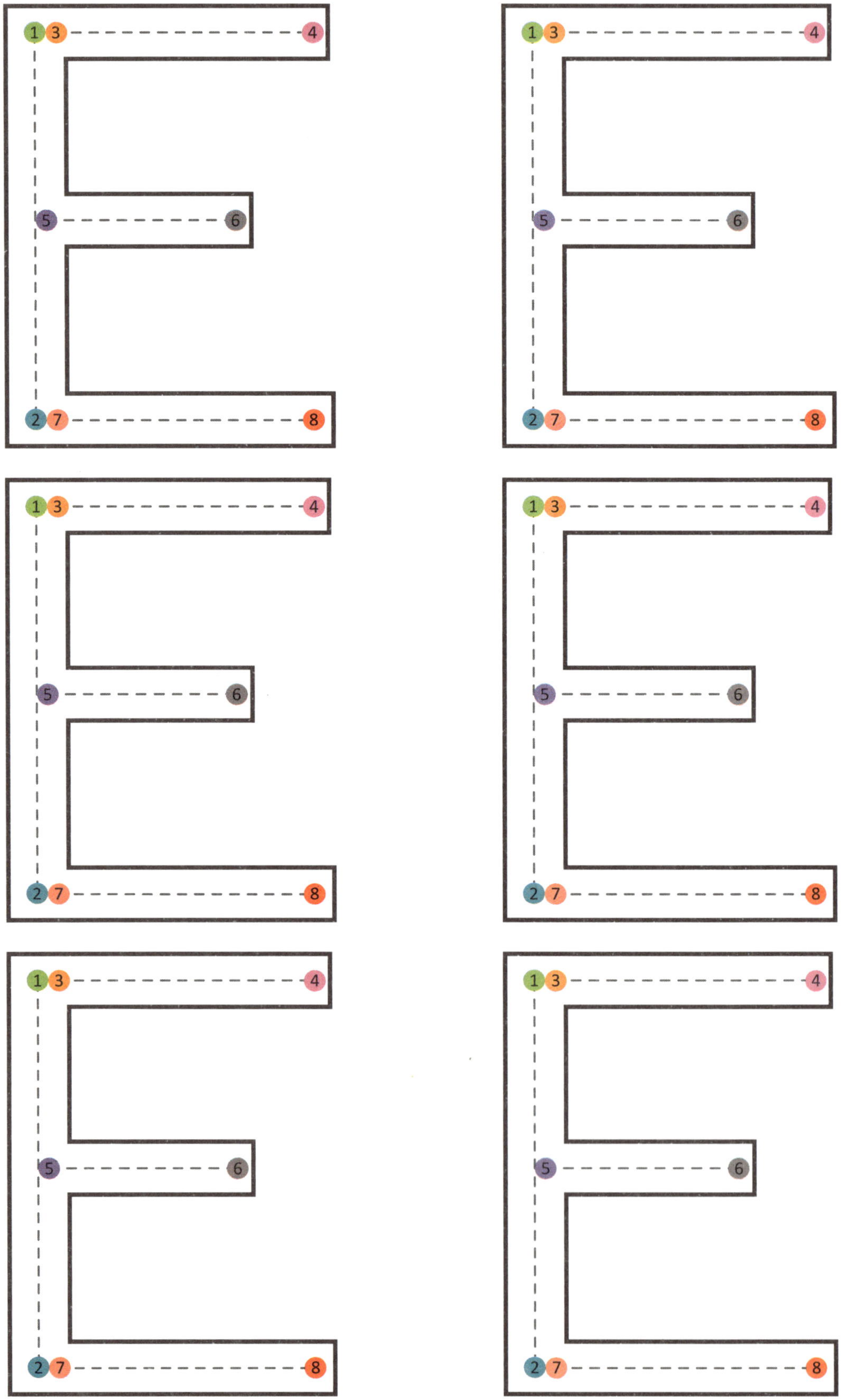

ENVELOPE

ELEPHANT

ELF

EGG

EGGPLANT

EAGLE

FARM

FIRE

FLAG

FISH

FLOWER

FEATHER

FRIENDLY LETTER F

TRACE OVER THE SMART DOTS TO MAKE LETTER F AND RECOGNISE THESE ASSOCIATED OBJECTS.

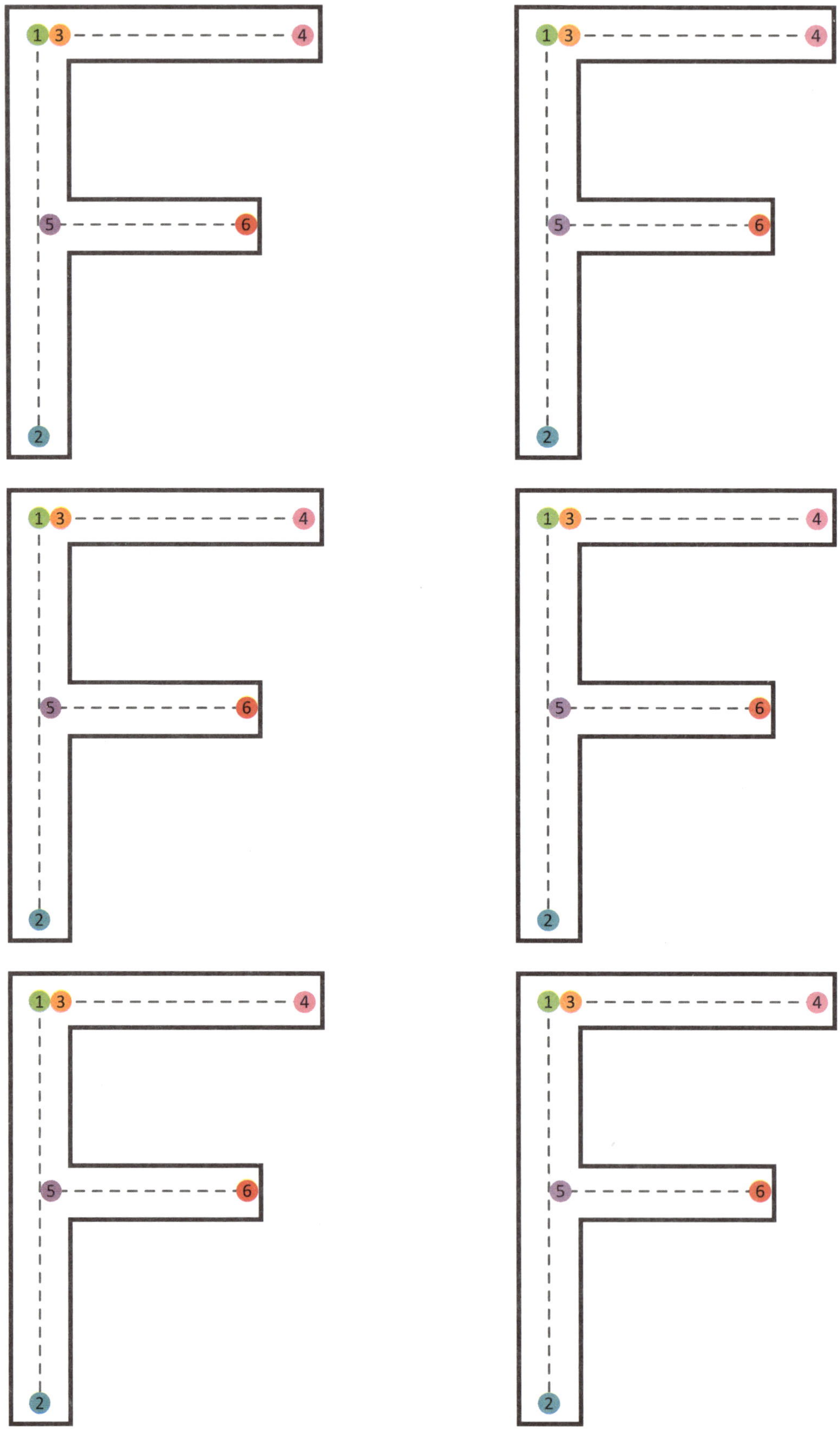

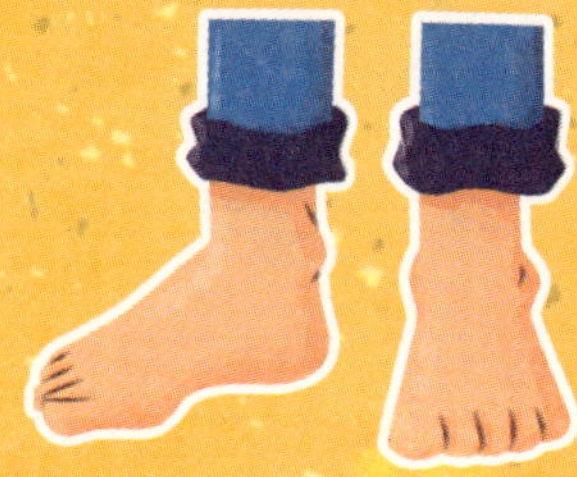

FEET

FORK

FLAMINGO

FOOTBALL

FOLDER

FOX

HELPFUL LETTER H

TRACE OVER THE SMART DOTS TO MAKE LETTER H AND RECOGNISE THESE ASSOCIATED OBJECTS.

HORSE

HOUSE

HAMMER

HARP

HELICOPTER

HEN

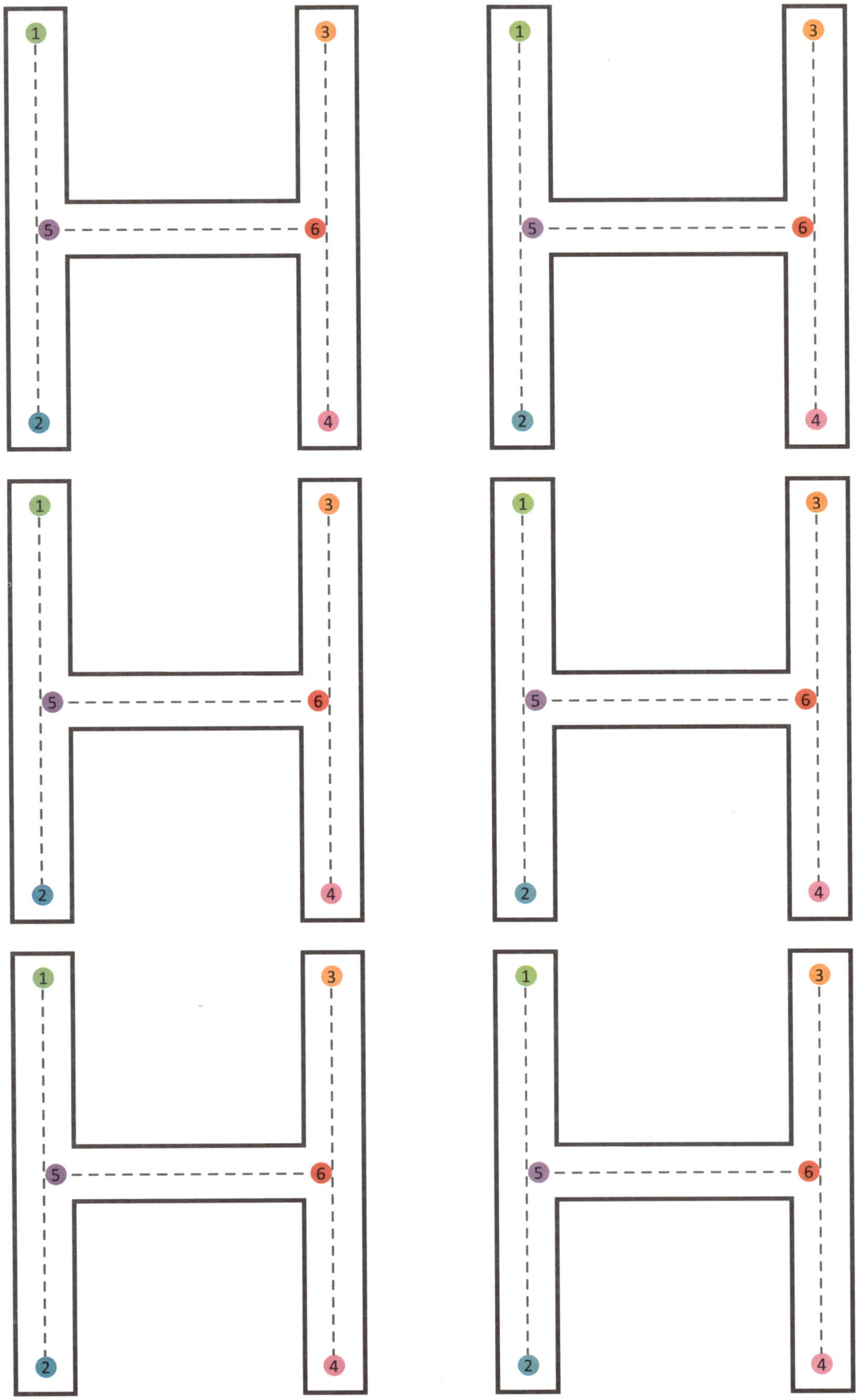

HIPPOPOTAMUS

HONEY

HAT

HANDBAG

HEART

HELMET

KETTLE

KEY

KIWI

KANGAROO

KITE

KITCHEN

KIND LETTER K

TRACE OVER THE SMART DOTS TO MAKE LETTER K AND RECOGNISE THESE ASSOCIATED OBJECTS.

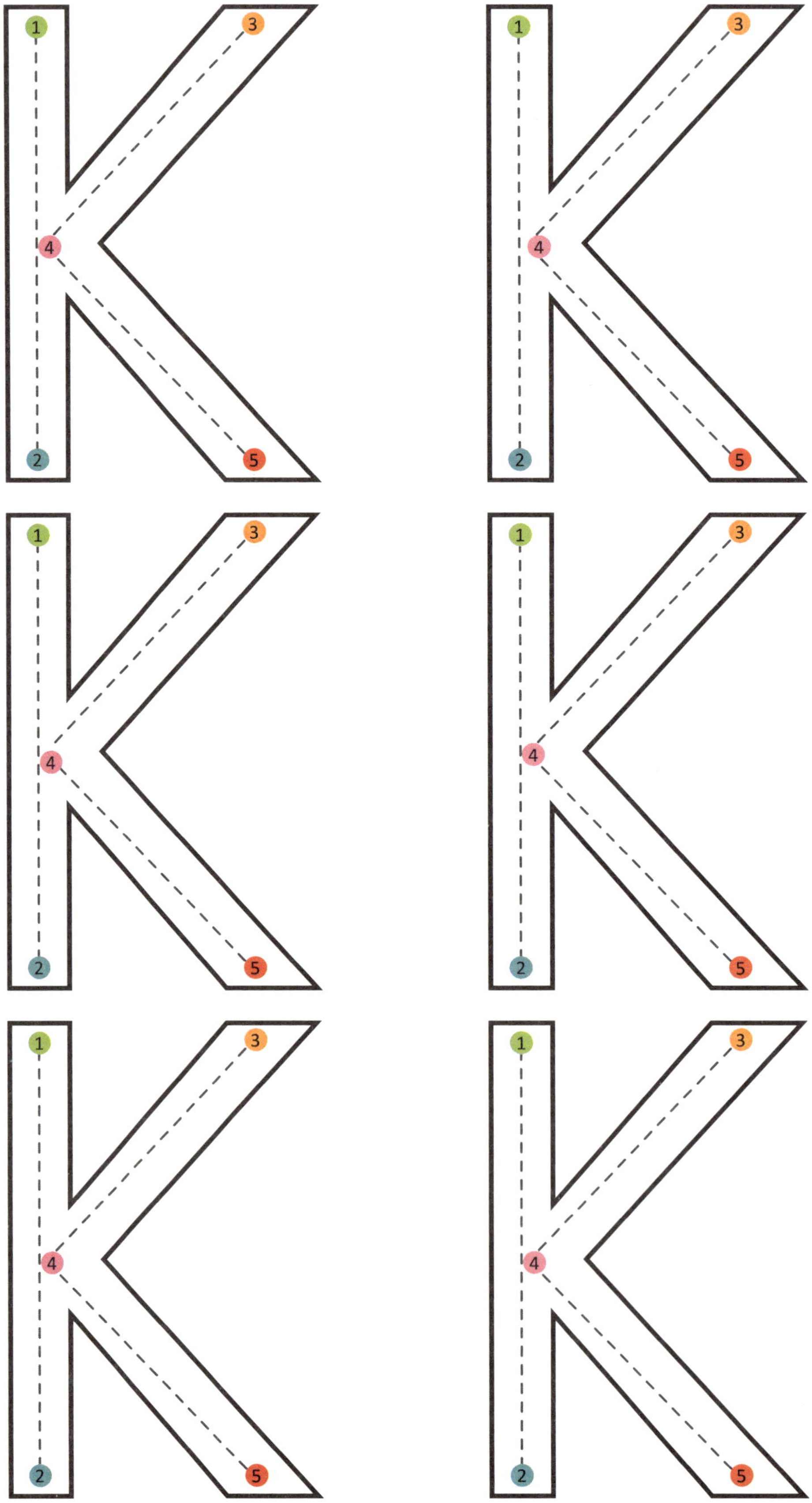

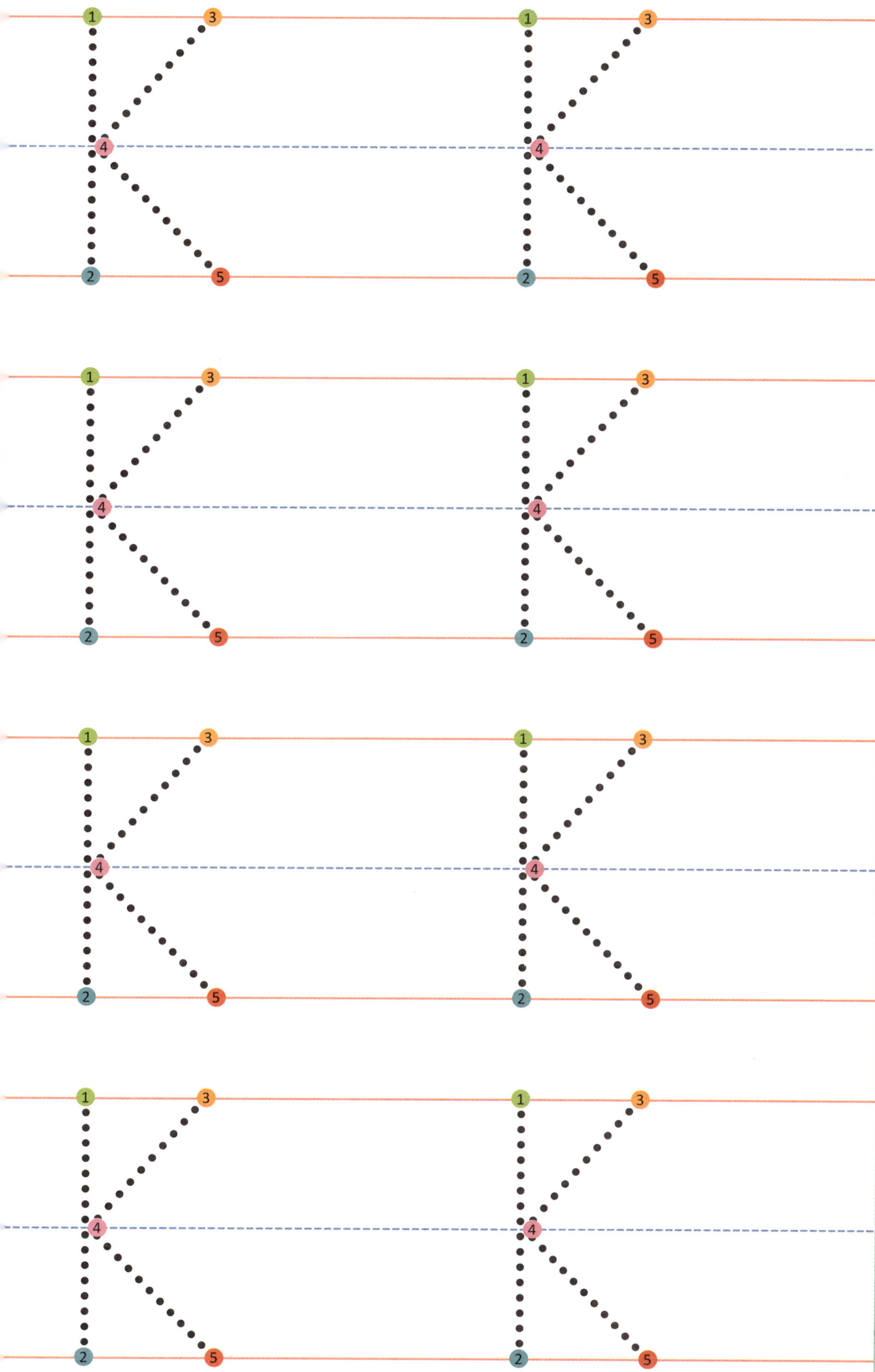

KITTEN

KENYA

KETCHUP

KOALA

KAYAK

KING

ADVENTUROUS LETTER A

TRACE OVER THE SMART DOTS TO MAKE LETTER A AND RECOGNISE THESE ASSOCIATED OBJECTS.

APPLE

AVOCADO

APE

ALLIGATOR

ANT

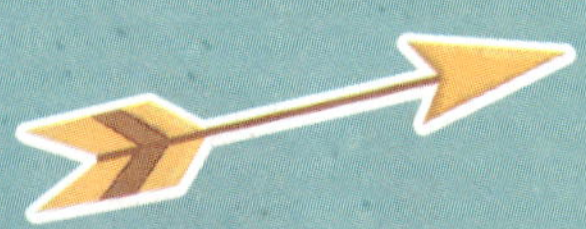

ARROW

ARM

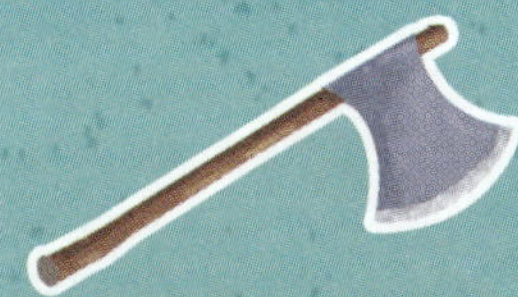

AXE

AIRPLANE

AIRPORT

AMBULANCE

ANCHOR

VIBRANT LETTER V

TRACE OVER THE SMART DOTS TO MAKE LETTER V AND RECOGNISE THESE ASSOCIATED OBJECTS.

VEGETABLES

VALLEY

VIOLIN

VIDEO GAME

VULTURE

VOLCANO

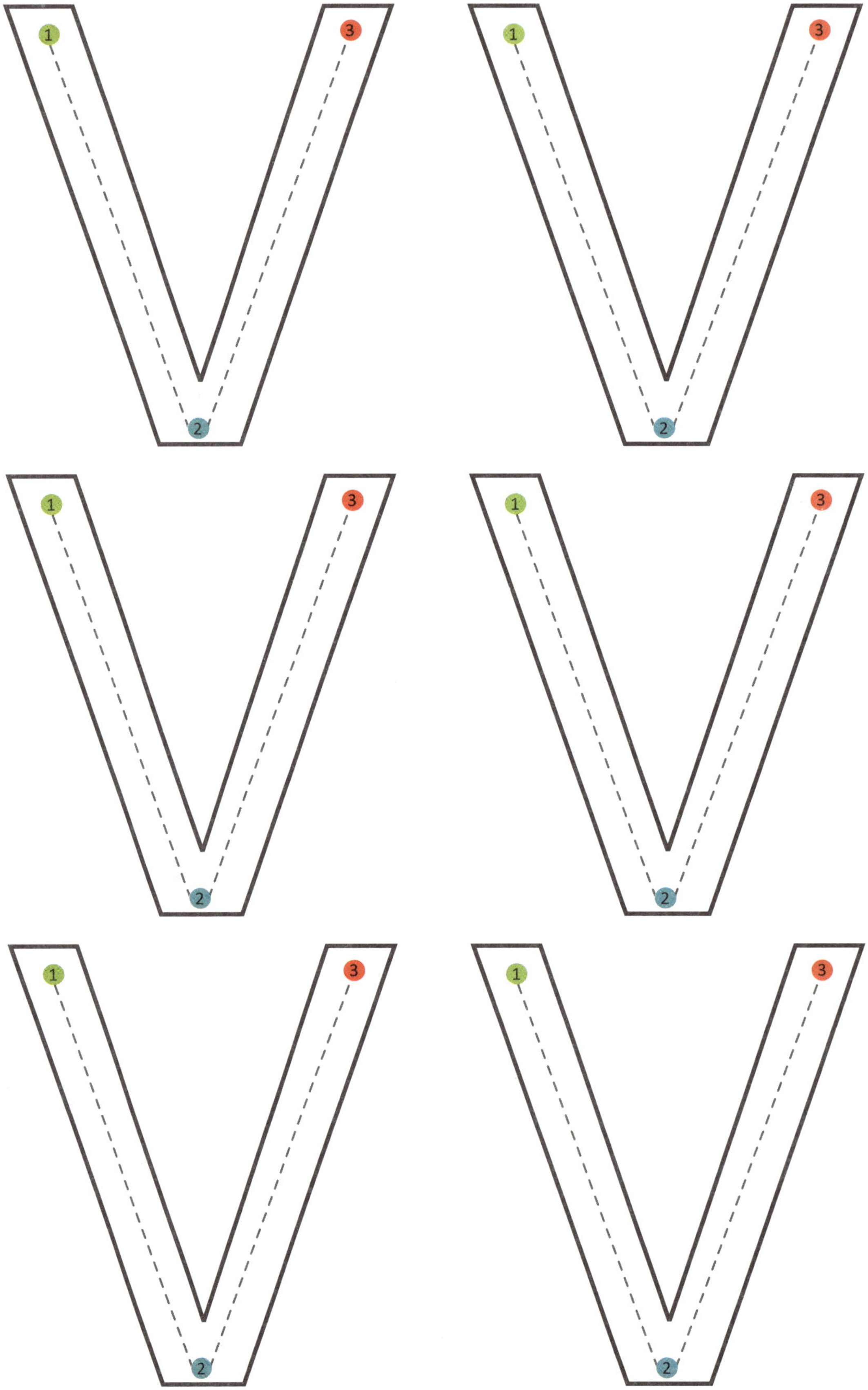

VOLLEYBALL

VASE

VACCINE

VEST

VILLAGE

VAN

WINDOW

WATER

WATERMELON

WAFFLE

WOLF

WHALE

WITTY LETTER W

TRACE OVER THE SMART DOTS TO MAKE LETTER W AND RECOGNISE THESE ASSOCIATED OBJECTS.

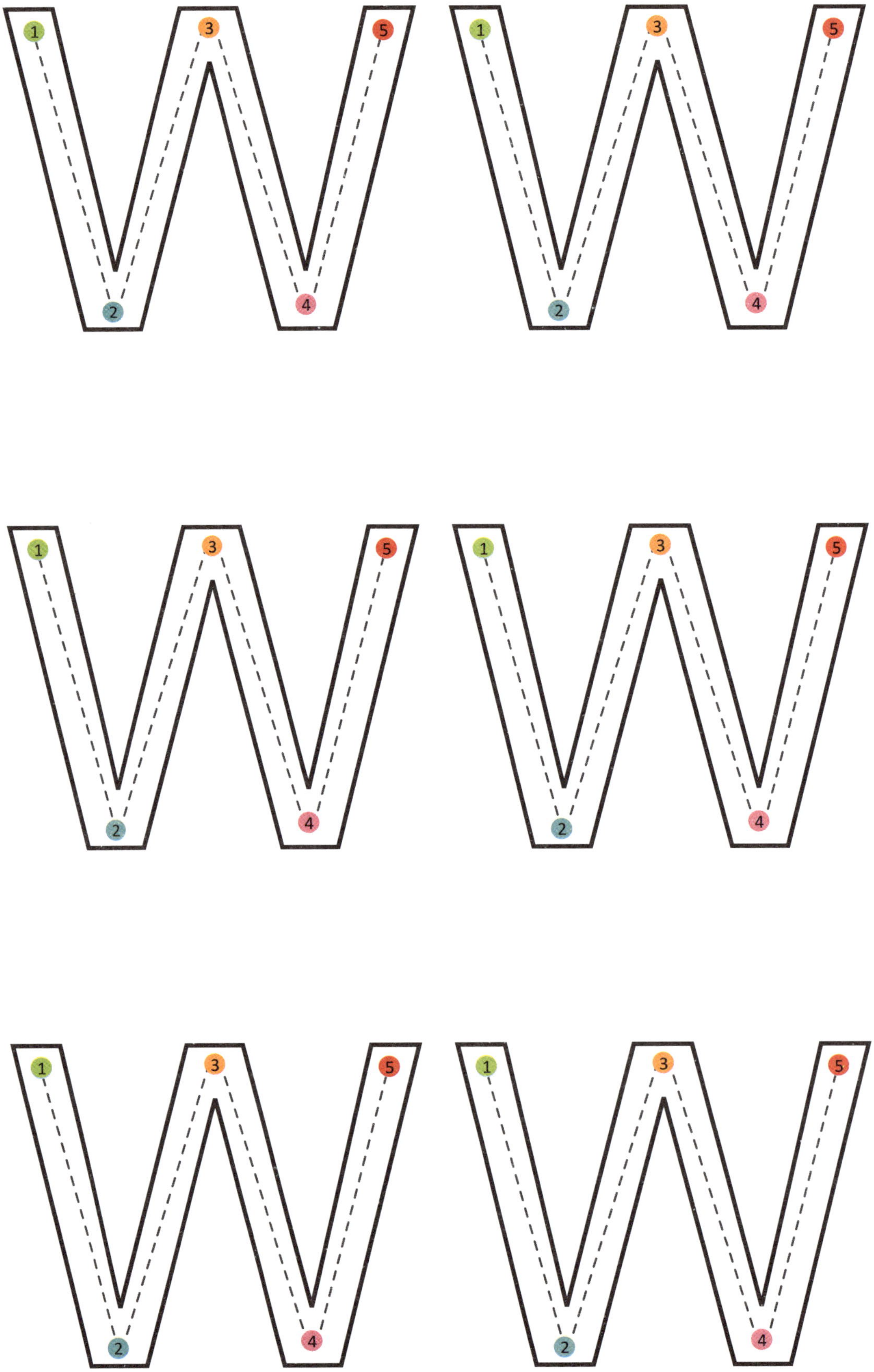

WATCH

WHISTLE

WHEEL

WALRUS

WORM

WALNUT

XENIAL LETTER X

TRACE OVER THE SMART DOTS TO MAKE LETTER X AND RECOGNISE THESE ASSOCIATED OBJECTS.

XYLOPHONE

X-RAY

X-RAY FISH

X-MAS TREE

XEROX MACHINE

XERUS

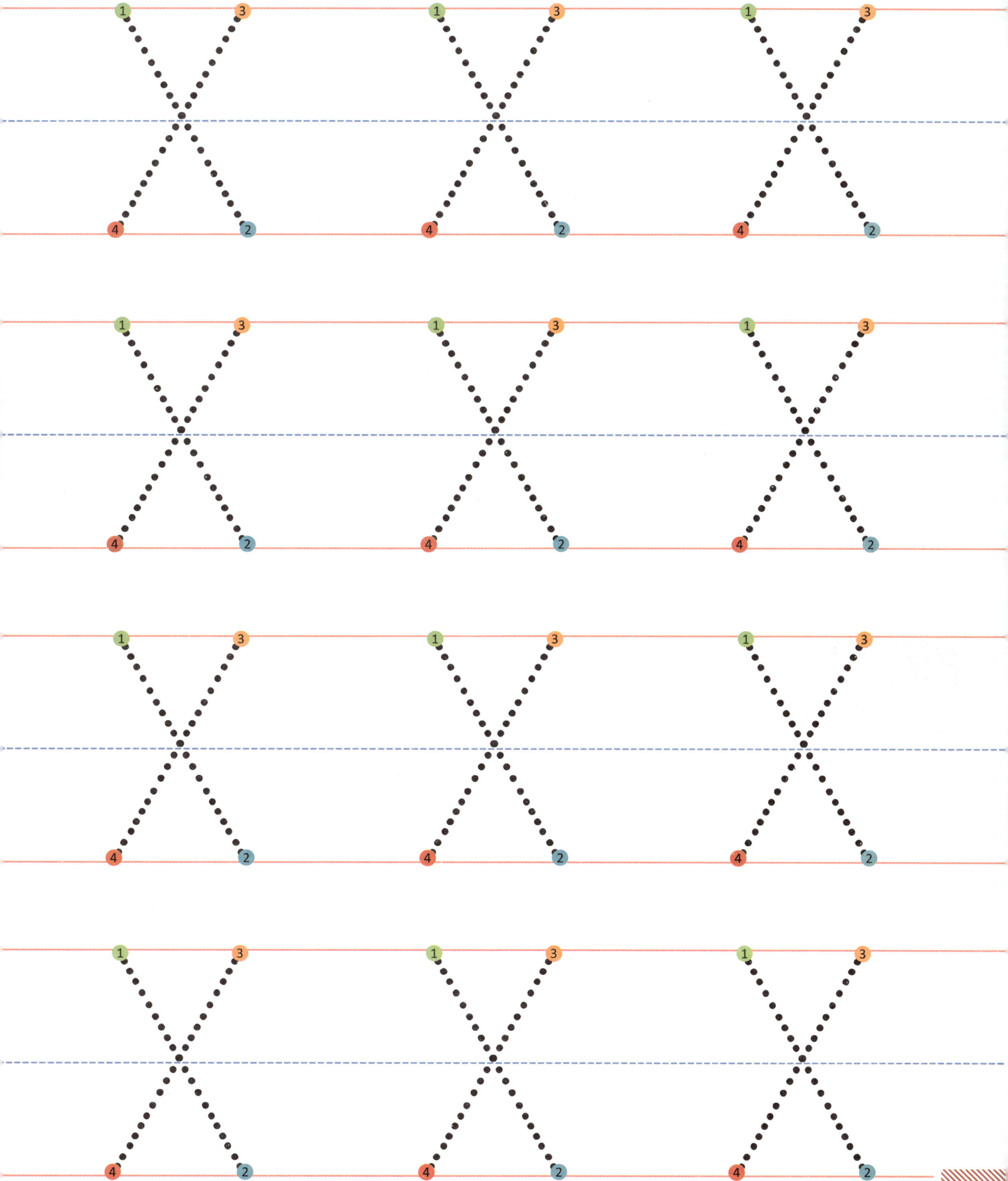
1
2
3
4

YO-YO

YELLOW

YOGURT

YAK

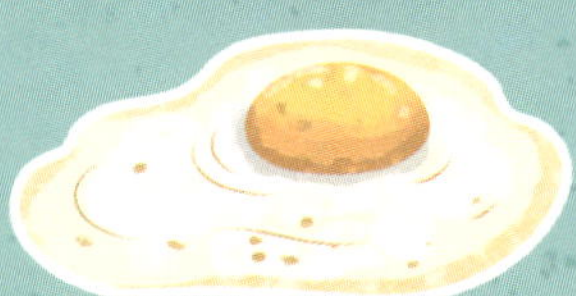

YOLK

YARN

YUMMY LETTER Y

TRACE OVER THE SMART DOTS TO MAKE LETTER Y AND RECOGNISE THESE ASSOCIATED OBJECTS.

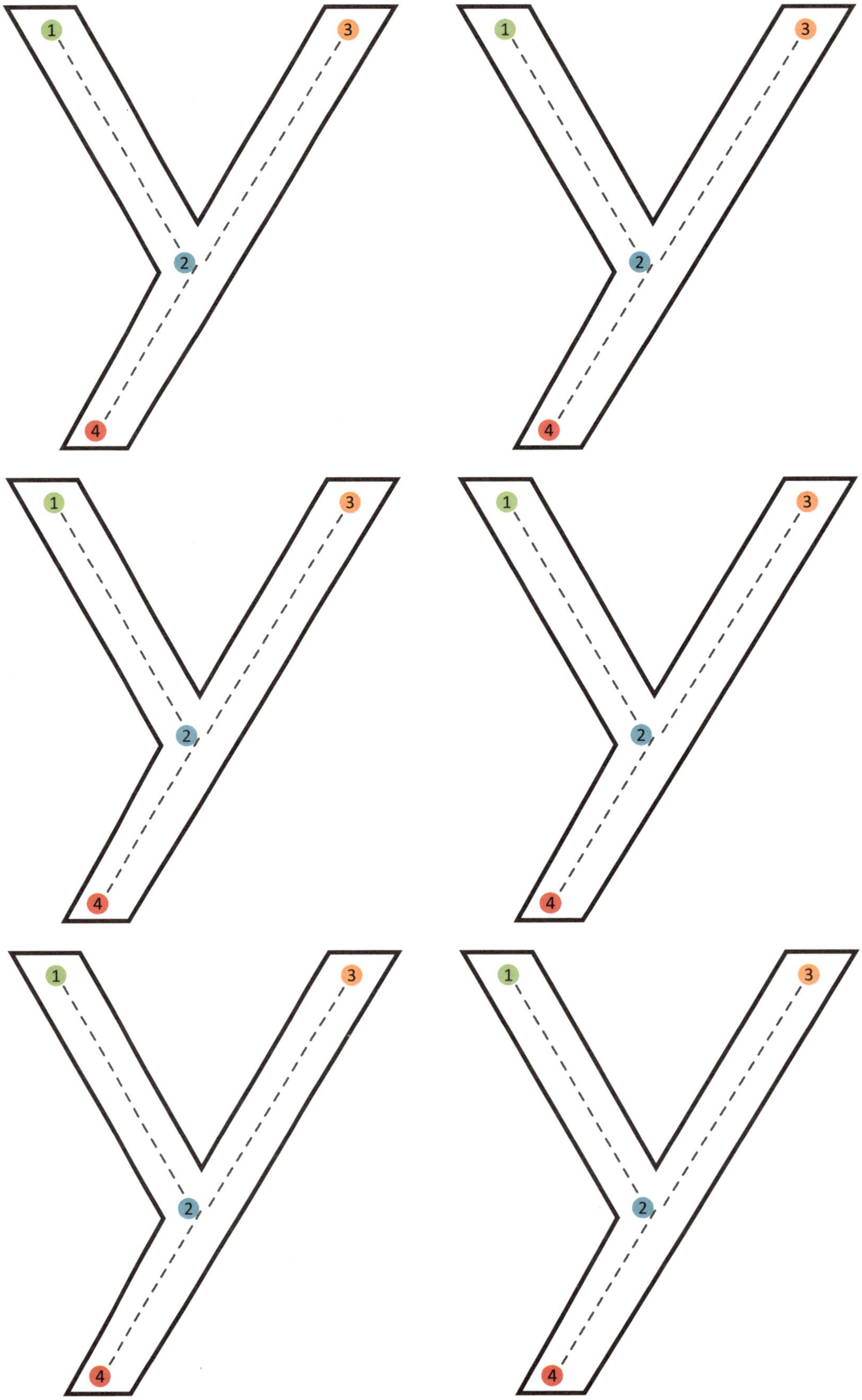

YOGA

YAM

YACHT

YUZU

YETI

YAWN

MAGICAL LETTER M

TRACE OVER THE SMART DOTS TO MAKE LETTER M AND RECOGNISE THESE ASSOCIATED OBJECTS.

MILK

MUG

MONKEY

MOON

MOTORCYCLE

MANGO

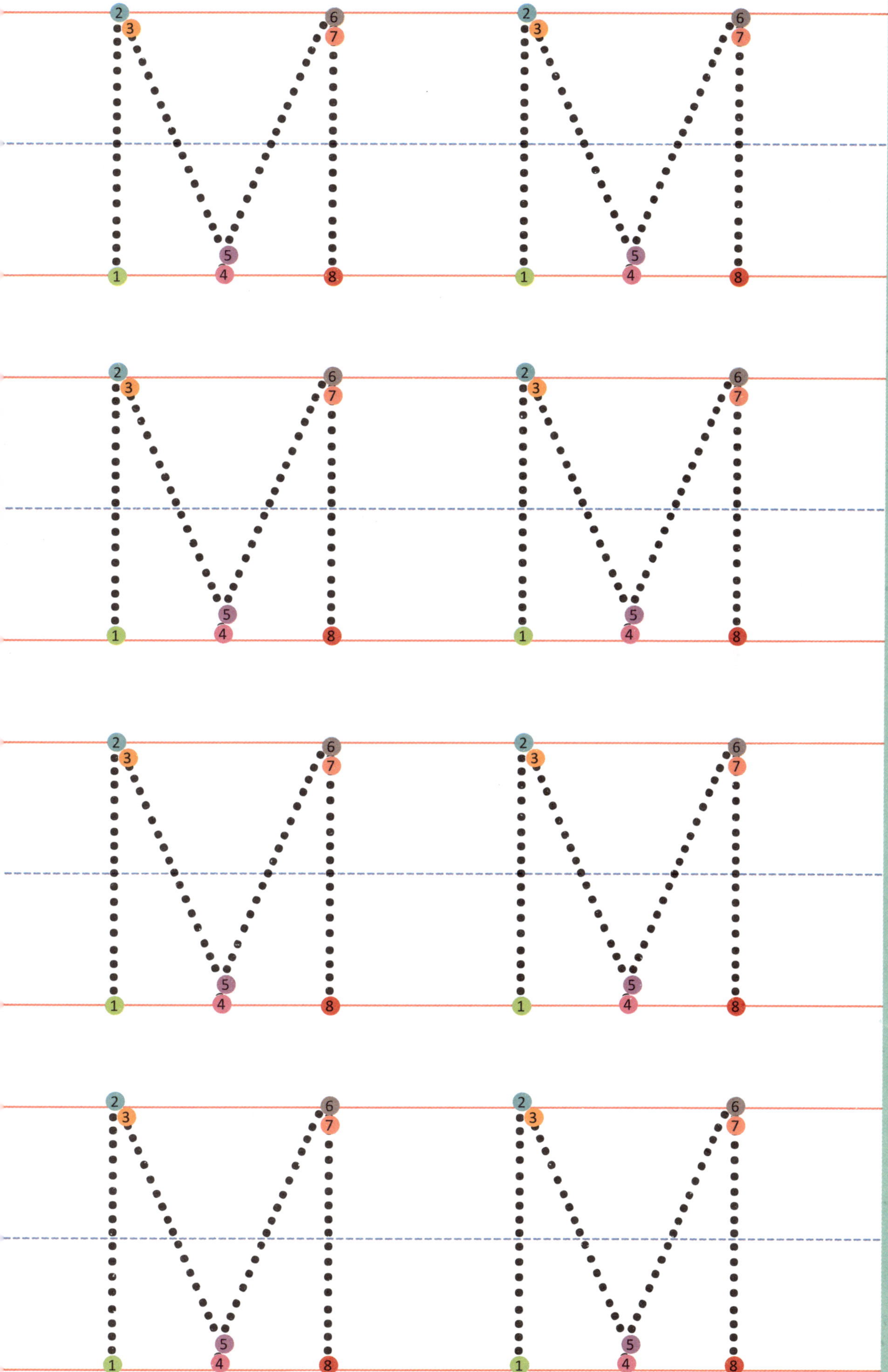

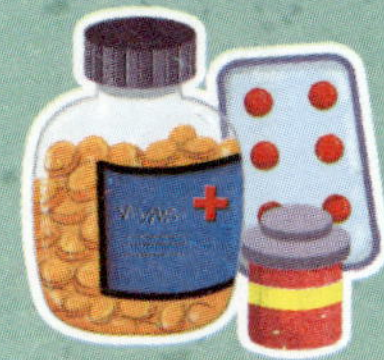

MEDICINE

MIRROR

MUSHROOM

MOUSE

MARSHMALLOW

MOP

NET

NEWSPAPER

NOODLE

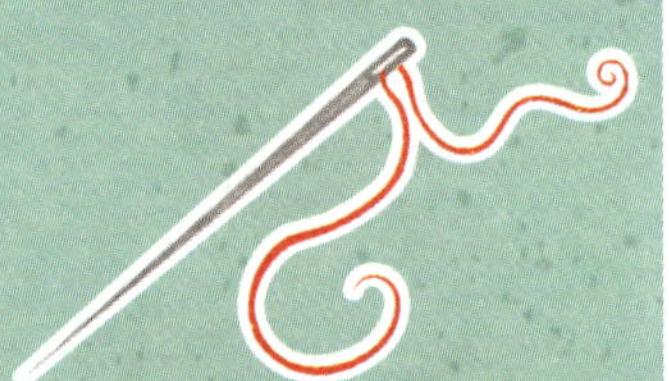

NEEDLE

NAPKIN

NIGHT

NECESSARY LETTER N

TRACE OVER THE SMART DOTS TO MAKE LETTER N AND RECOGNISE THESE ASSOCIATED OBJECTS.

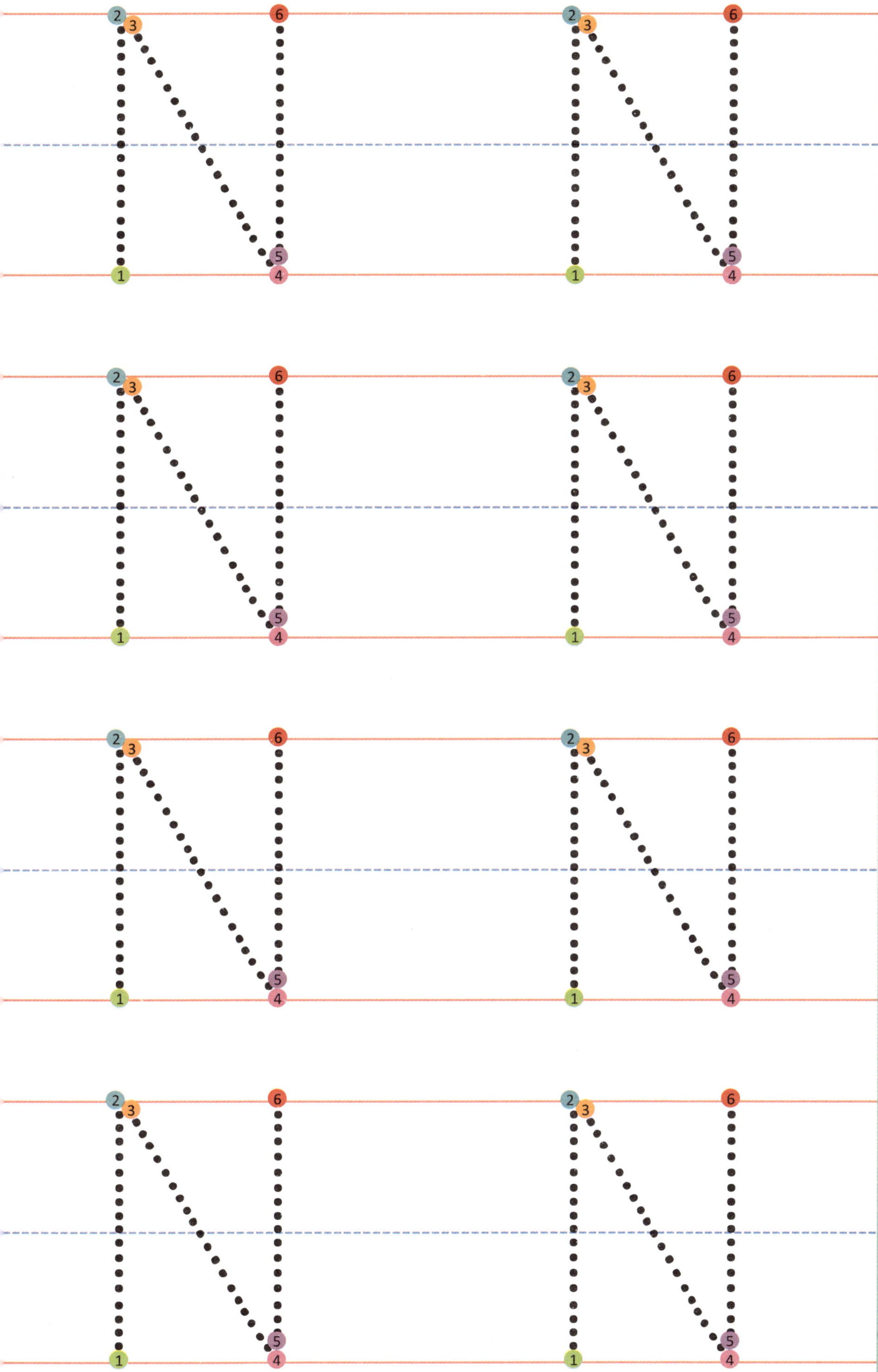

NECKLACE

NEST

NOTEBOOK

NUTS

NOSE

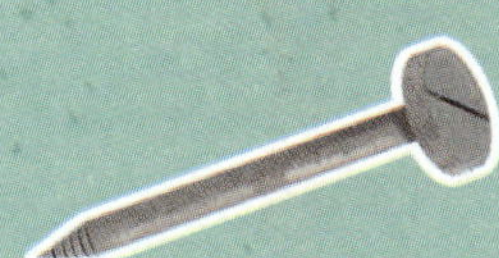

NAIL

ZOO

ZIG-ZAG

ZIPLOCK BAG

ZEBRA CROSSING

ZEBRA

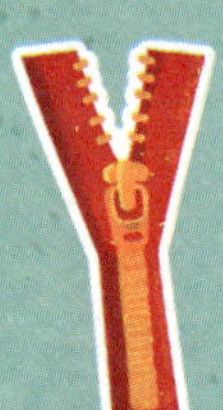

ZIP

ZESTY LETTER Z

TRACE OVER THE SMART DOTS TO MAKE LETTER Z AND RECOGNISE THESE ASSOCIATED OBJECTS.

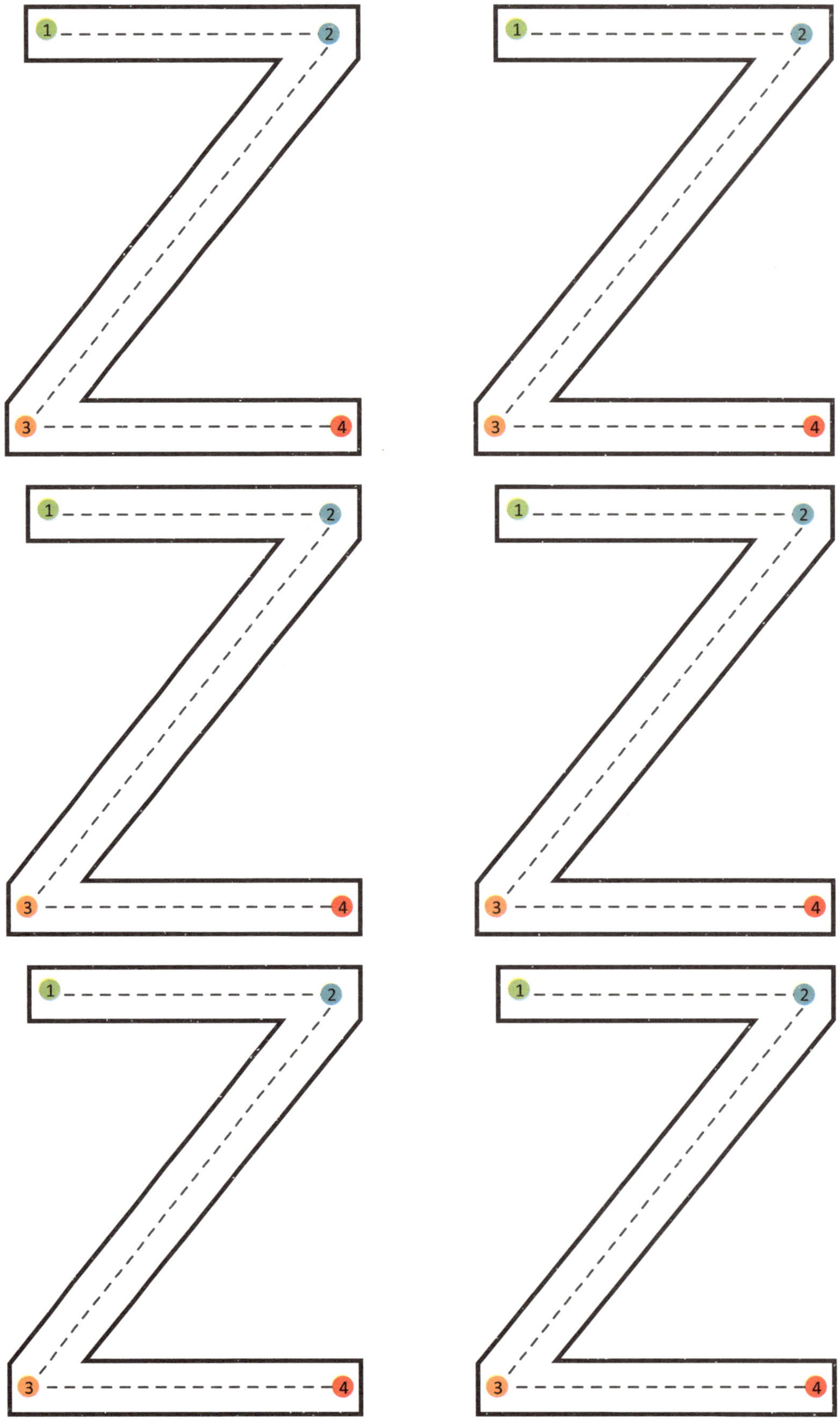

ZEBRA SHARK

ZIP LINE

ZOMBIE

ZUCCHINI

ZERO

ZEPPELIN

CARING LETTER C

TRACE OVER THE SMART DOTS TO MAKE LETTER C AND RECOGNISE THESE ASSOCIATED OBJECTS.

CABBAGE

CAKE

CANDY

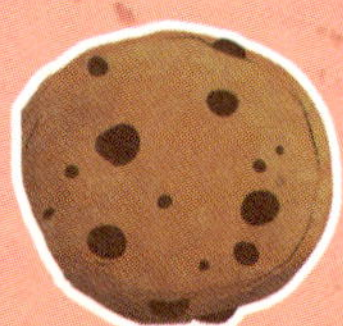

COOKIE

CATERPILLAR

COW

CLOUD

CROW

CAMERA

CORN

CANDLE

CARPET

OWL

OSTRICH

OCTOPUS

ONION

ORANGE

OIL

OBEDIENT LETTER O

TRACE OVER THE SMART DOTS TO MAKE LETTER O AND RECOGNISE THESE ASSOCIATED OBJECTS.

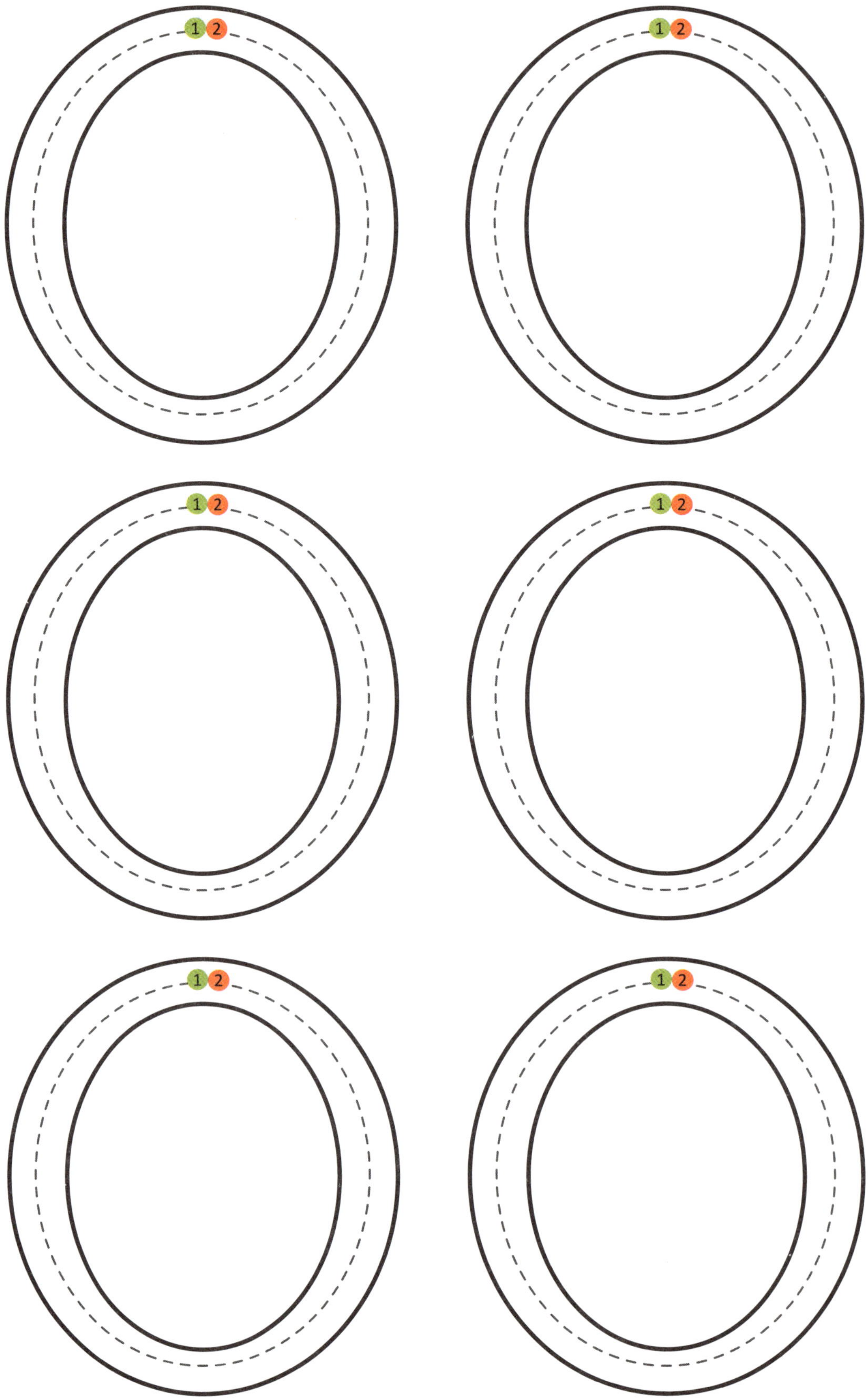

OCEAN

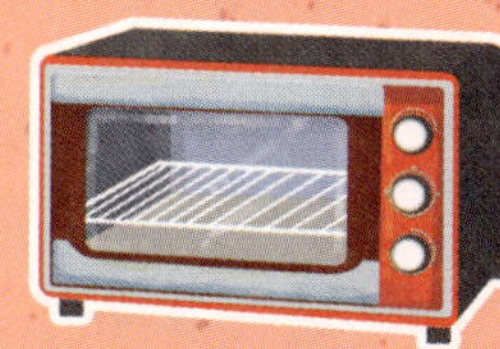

OVEN

OMLET

ORIGAMI

OX

OYSTER

QUEEN

QUILT

QUILL

QUESTION MARK

QUAIL

QUEUE

QUIRKY LETTER Q

TRACE OVER THE SMART DOTS TO MAKE LETTER Q AND RECOGNISE THESE ASSOCIATED OBJECTS.

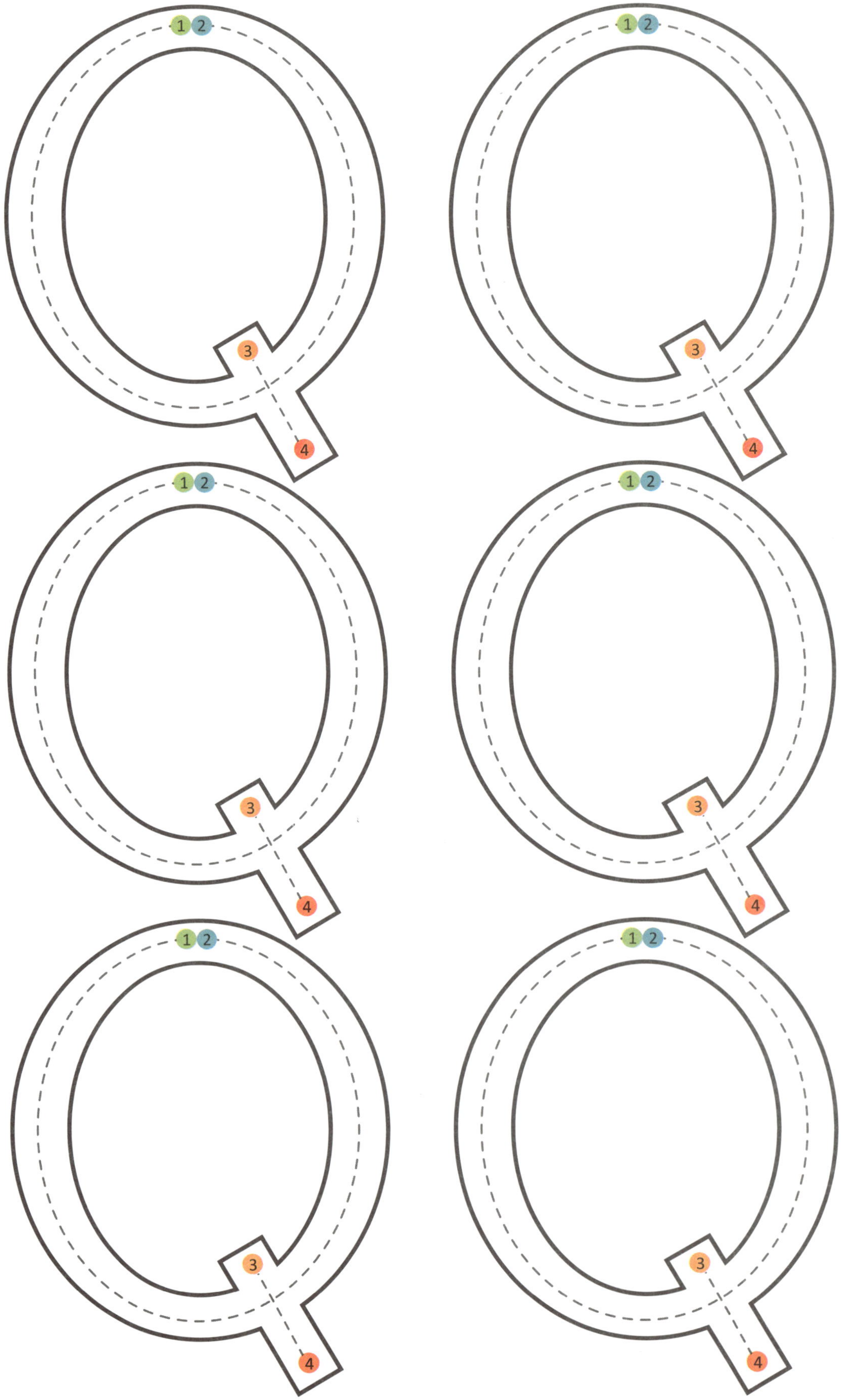

QUINOA

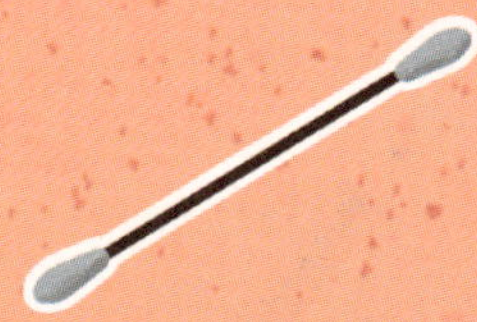

Q-TIP

QUIET

QUOTE

QATAR

QUIZ

PARROT

PENCIL

POT

PIG

PENGUIN

PLANT

PLAYFUL LETTER P

TRACE OVER THE SMART DOTS TO MAKE LETTER P AND RECOGNISE THESE ASSOCIATED OBJECTS.

PARACHUTE

PANDA

PINEAPPLE

PUMPKIN

PIZZA

PEA

RELAXED LETTER R

TRACE OVER THE SMART DOTS TO MAKE LETTER R AND RECOGNISE THESE ASSOCIATED OBJECTS.

RAINBOW

ROCKET

RICE

RING

RAIN

RABBIT

ROSE

RHINOCEROS

ROBOT

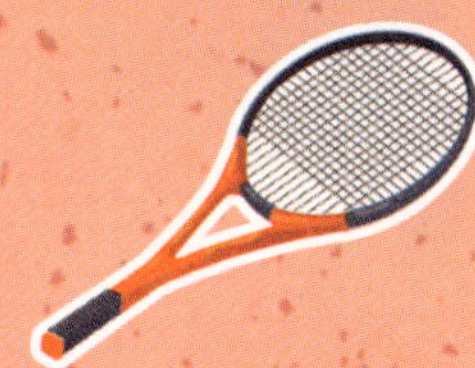

RACKET

ROAD

RAT

DOLL

DESK

DICE

DOLPHIN

DONUT

DRUM

DELIGHTFUL LETTER D

TRACE OVER THE SMART DOTS TO MAKE LETTER D AND RECOGNISE THESE ASSOCIATED OBJECTS.

DUCK

DUSTER

DUSTBIN

DOOR

DOG

DRAGON

BEE

BRUSH

BIRD

BUFFALO

BOOK

BAG

BRILLIANT LETTER B

TRACE OVER THE SMART DOTS TO MAKE LETTER B AND RECOGNISE THESE ASSOCIATED OBJECTS.

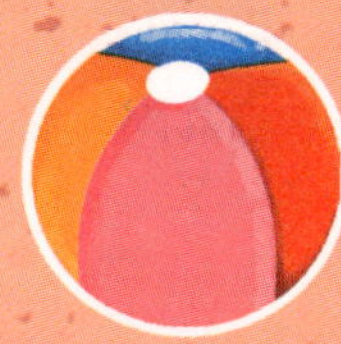

BALL

BASKET

BOTTLE

BATHTUB

BLACK

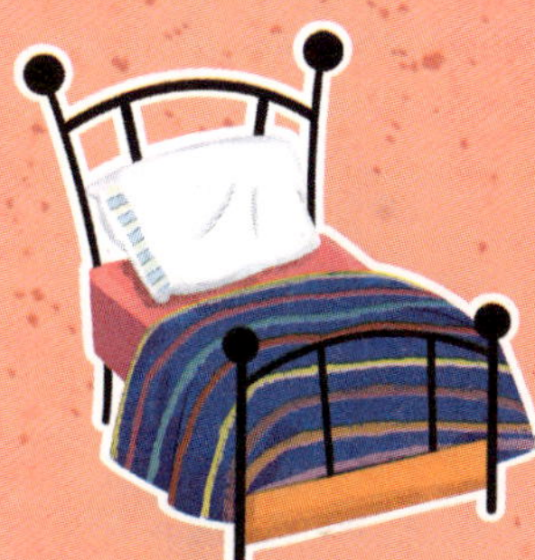

BED

JOYFUL LETTER J

TRACE OVER THE SMART DOTS TO MAKE LETTER J AND RECOGNISE THESE ASSOCIATED OBJECTS.

JAM

JELLYFISH

JET

JUG

JELLY

JUICE

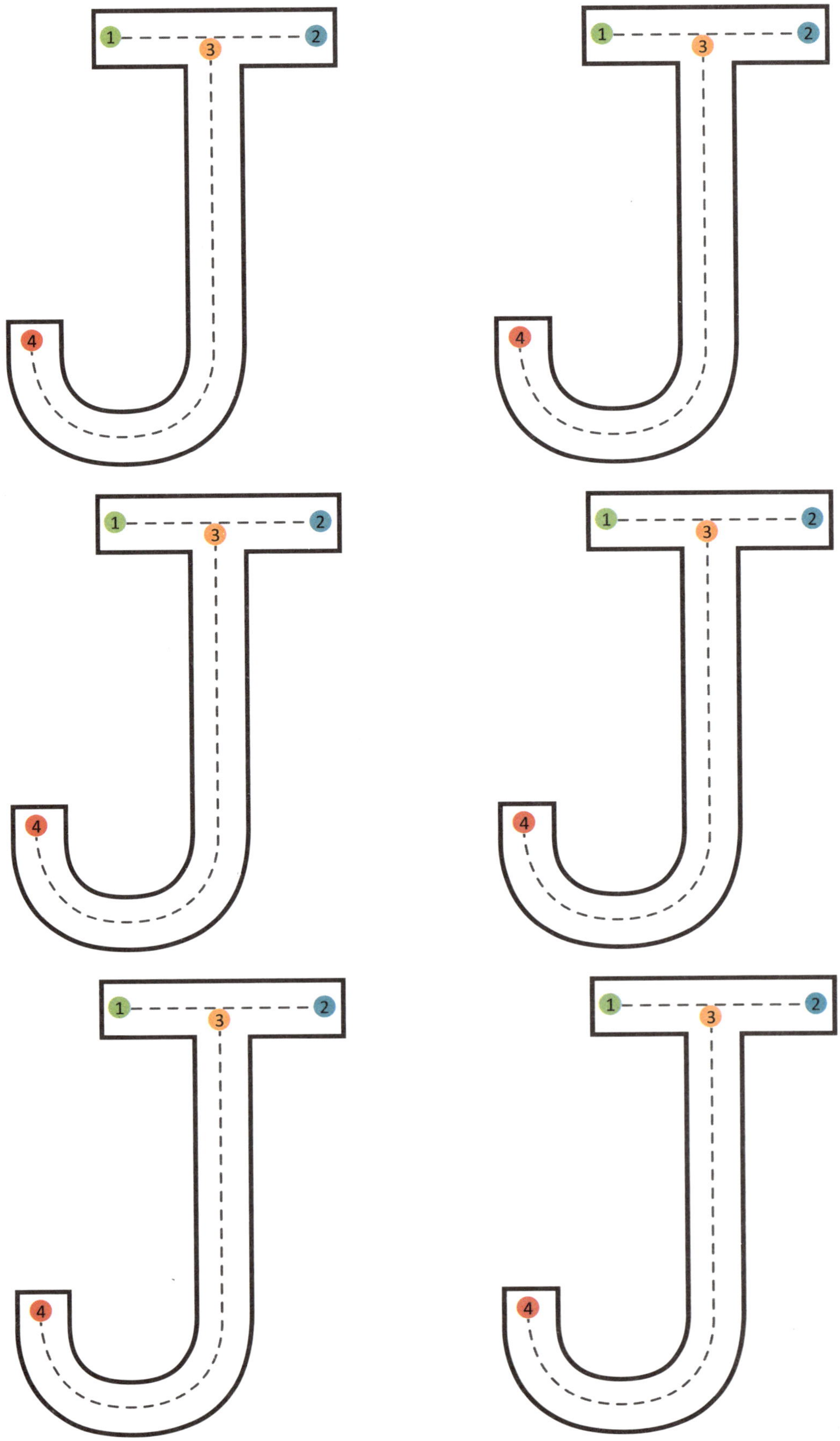

JAGUAR

JACKFRUIT

JACKET

JEANS

JEEP

JUNGLE

UMBRELLA

UP

UNIFORM

UNICORN

UNDER GARMENTS

URN

UNSTOPPABLE LETTER U

TRACE OVER THE SMART DOTS TO MAKE LETTER U AND RECOGNISE THESE ASSOCIATED OBJECTS.

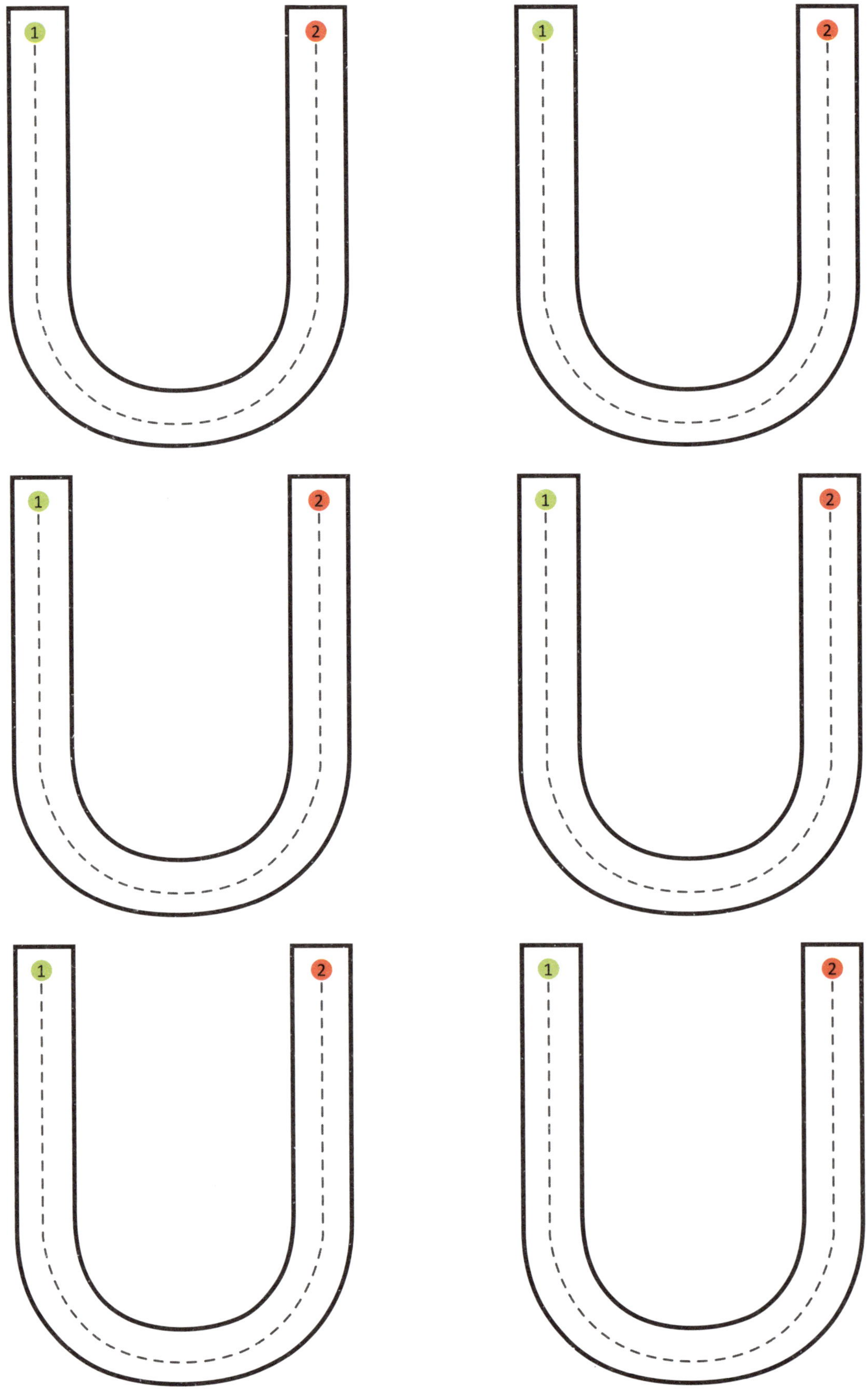

UTENSILS

U-TURN

URANUS

USB DRIVE

UNITED STATES OF AMERICA

UMPIRE

SHEEP

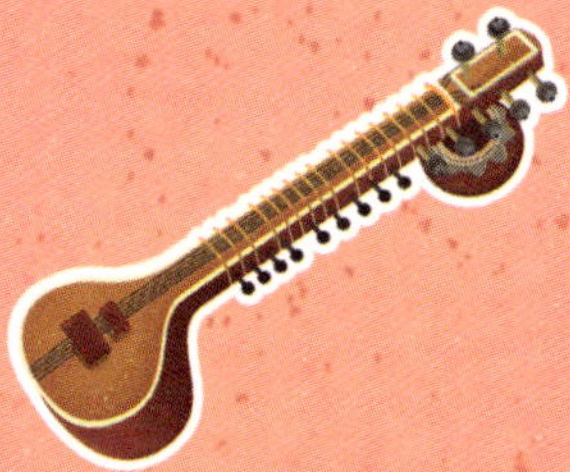
SITAR

SNAKE

SHIP

STARFISH

SUN

STRONG LETTER S

TRACE OVER THE SMART DOTS TO MAKE LETTER S AND RECOGNISE THESE ASSOCIATED OBJECTS.

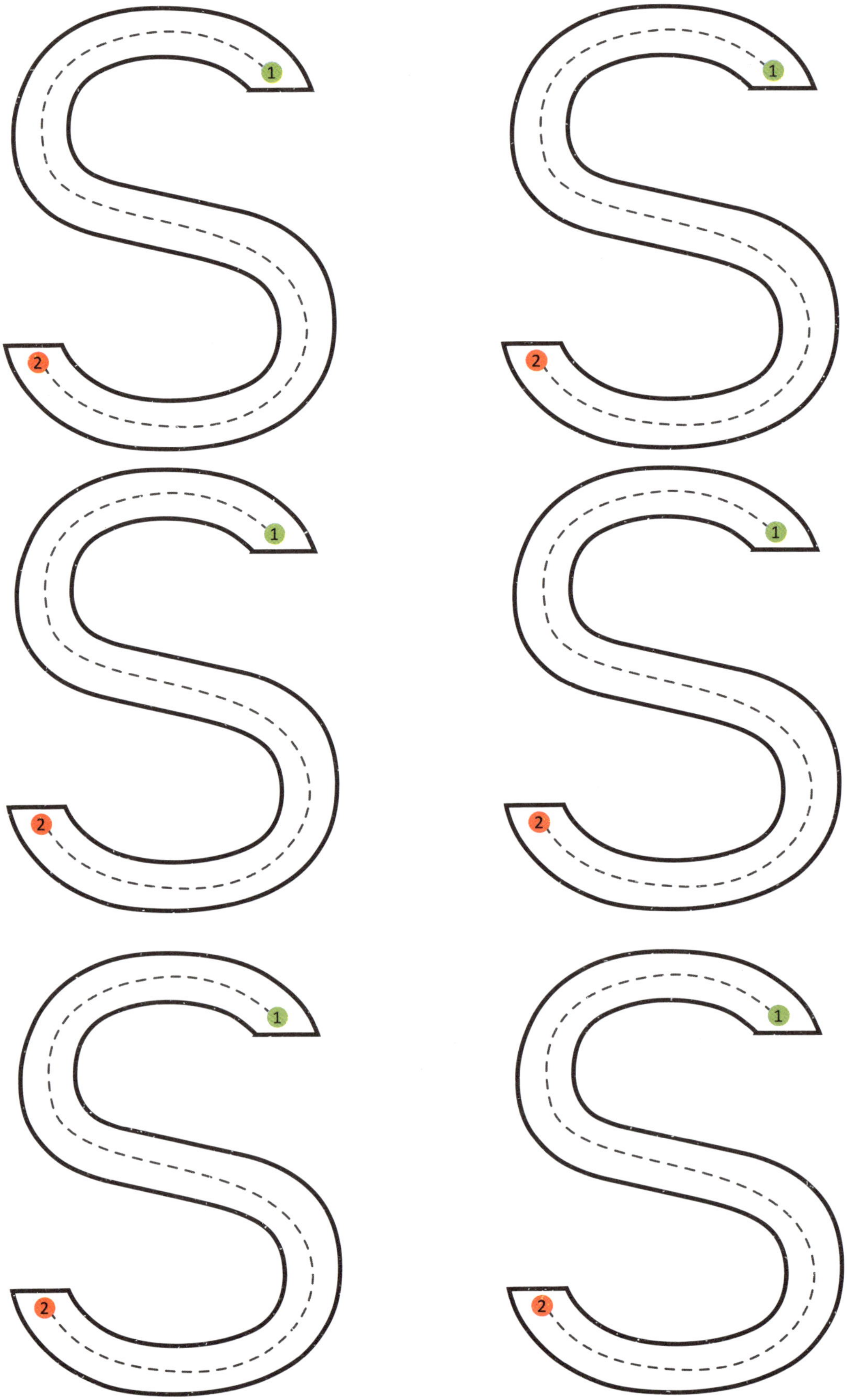

SHOES

STRAWBERRY

SOAP

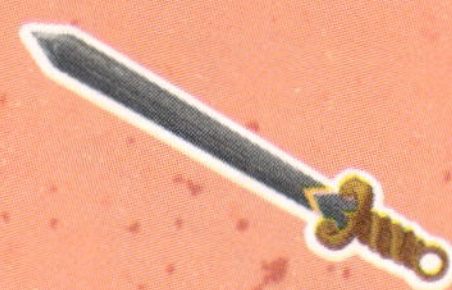

SWORD

SAND CASTLE

SHARK

GRASS

GOAT

GARAGE

GUITAR

GATE

GRAPES

GENEROUS LETTER G

TRACE OVER THE SMART DOTS TO MAKE LETTER G AND RECOGNISE THESE ASSOCIATED OBJECTS.

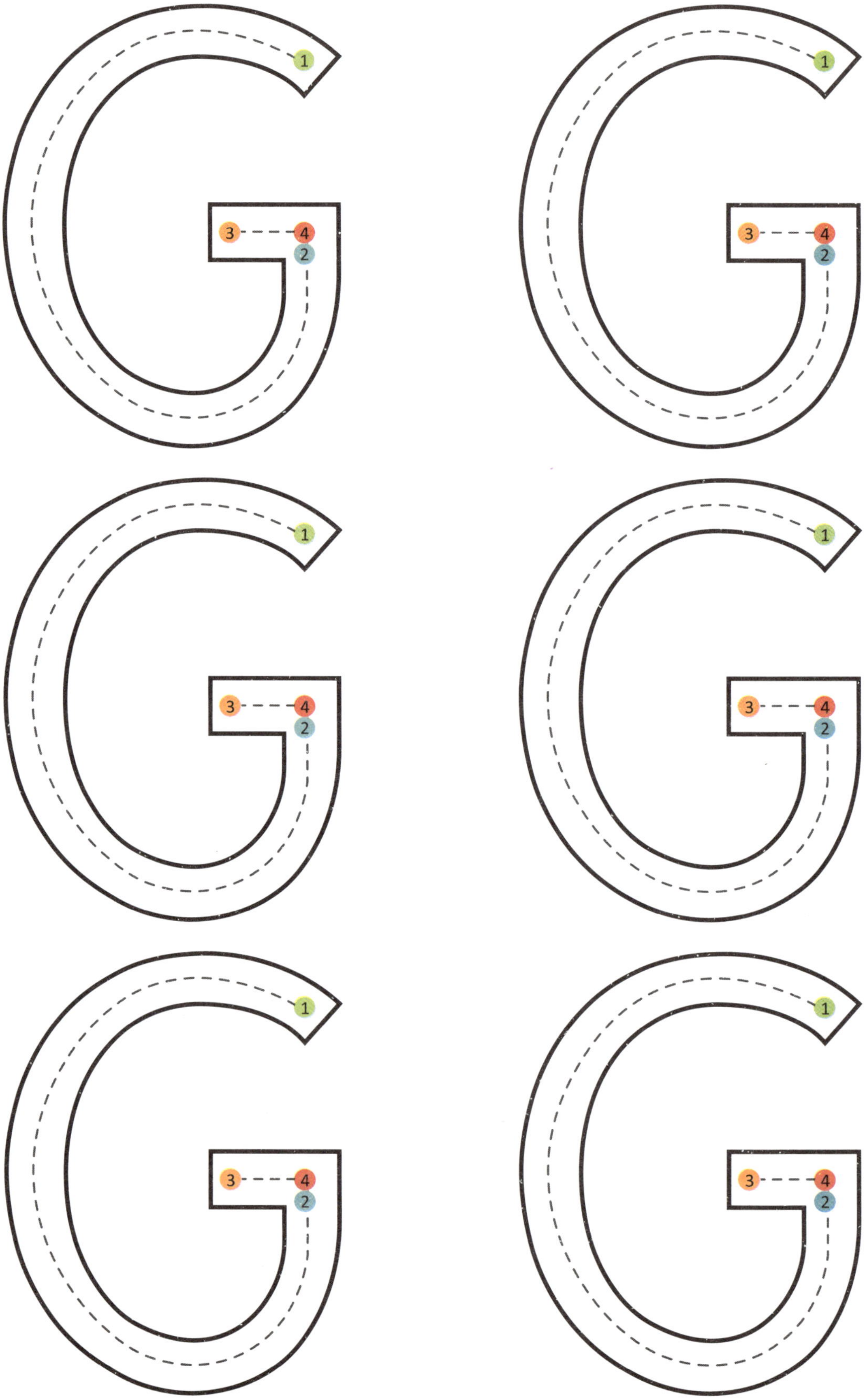

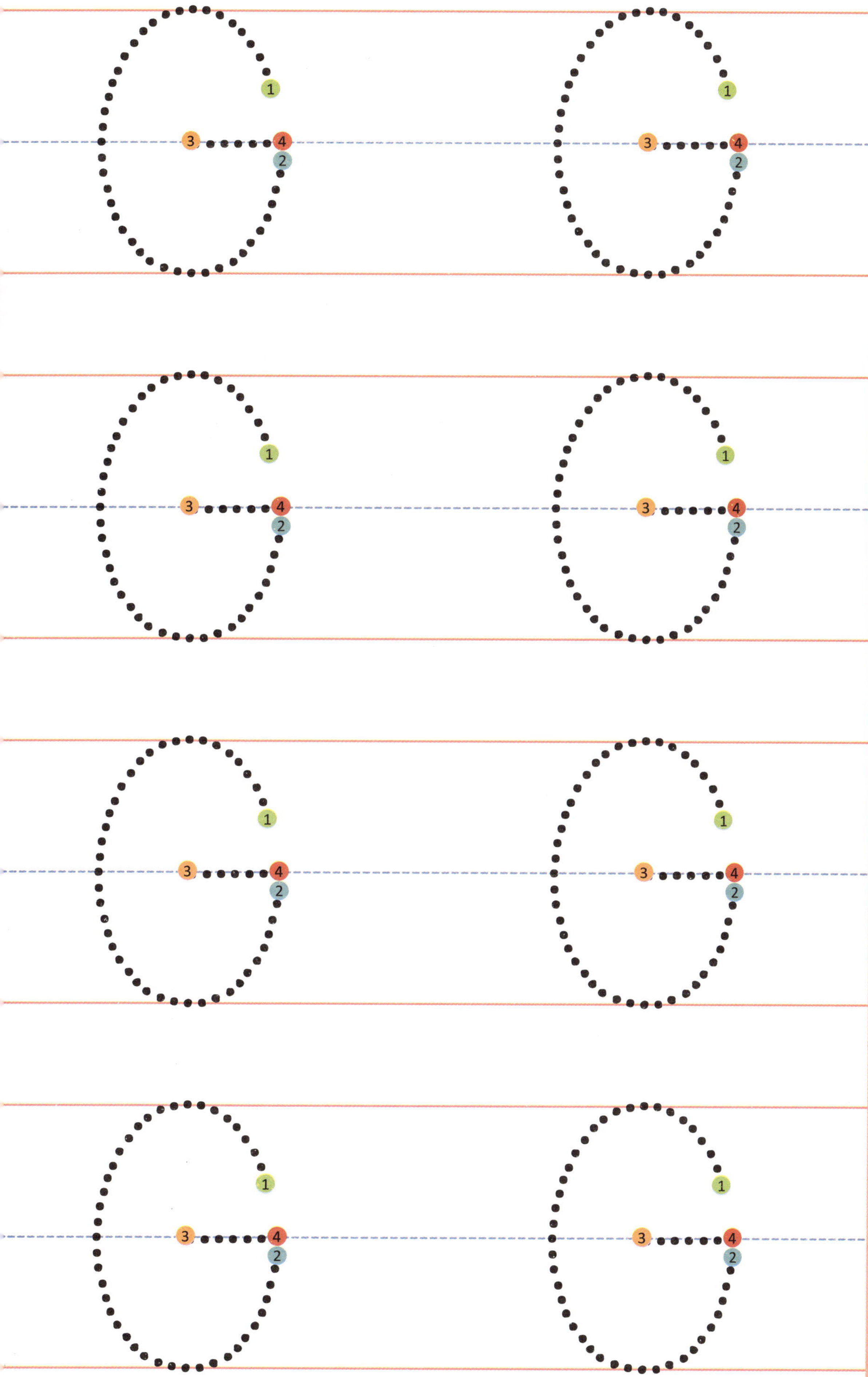

GORILLA

GIFT

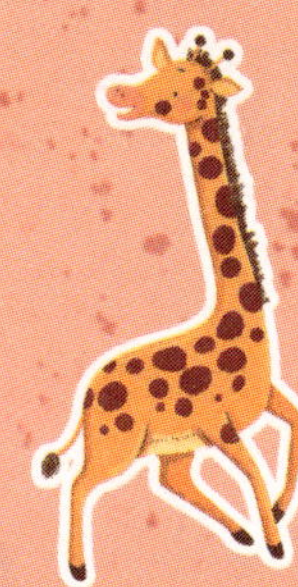

GIRAFFE

GOLDFISH

GLOBE

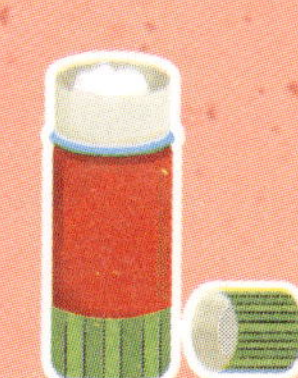

GLUE

Lil Legends

Certificate of

Achievement

This is to certify that .... has successfully completed the **Uppercase Tracing & Vocabulary Book.** He/She has also completed Level-1 of our Pre-writing Program.

OSWAAL BOOKS®
LEARNING MADE SIMPLE